Ann Coburn

THREE PLAYS
GET UP AND TIE YOUR FINGERS
SAFE
DEVIL'S GROUND

T0315847

OBERON BOOKS
LONDON

WWW.OBERONBOOKS.COM

THREE PLAYS

Contents

for John, Helen and Alex,
my faithful travelling audience

Preface

On the face of it, *Get Up and Tie Your Fingers, Safe* and *Devil's Ground* are three very different plays. *Get Up and Tie Your Fingers* deals with the lives of nineteenth century fishwives and herring lassies, *Safe* is a contemporary look at some of the dilemmas facing parents in the twenty-first century and *Devil's Ground* is a sixteenth century story of war and genocide. However, despite being centuries apart, the three plays have fundamental similarities. They all explore the same basic themes and each set of characters fight the same demons we all have to face – coping with death, dealing with guilt and learning to let our children go. All three plays also have their roots in story. *Get Up and Tie Your Fingers* is built around a story-telling spine in which the characters share the stories and myths of their own communities. *Safe* taps into deep shared roots of childhood and of story – specifically fairytales – in order to explore our contemporary parental fears for the safety of our children. In *Devil's Ground*, the stories and ballads of the reivers are prominent – and the power of myth and superstition helps to destroy the family.

Get Up and Tie Your Fingers was originally commissioned by the Borders Festival. My brief was to write a play about nineteenth century herring lasses and fishwives. This is a fascinating subject in itself. The life of a fishwife was founded on religion and superstition and dominated by the moods of the sea. Their days were filled with unrelenting work but they also loved songs and stories. The three women in a gutting crew formed bonds of friendship so strong, they lasted a lifetime. These remarkable women worked in the years when huge shoals of herring still journeyed around our coastline and the square russet sails of Fifies and Zulus filled our harbours. 'Get up and tie your fingers!' was the traditional cry of the caller, sent from the curing yards each morning during the herring season to rouse the gutting crews from their beds. The crews were strong, resilient women with financial independence, freedom of movement and an equal partnership with their men.

Jean, Molly and Janet are three such women, but they also have more personal stories to tell. Mollie yearns to get away from the village, Jean wants to keep her safe at home. Like all mothers and daughters, they are the closest of enemies. Jean has a secret, hidden deep in her past and she can never let Molly go until she faces up to her own demons. Janet has enough humour, warmth, wisdom and determination to take on the worst of demons, but even Janet is unprepared for one terrible afternoon which changes everything. 'Black Friday', 14 October 1881.

Black Friday is the third thread running through the play. It is the story of one of the Borders' greatest ever tragedies – the Eyemouth fishing disaster of 1881. Forty five boats set out from Eyemouth harbour, principal port and heart of the Scottish Borders fishing industry. Only twenty five were to return. One hundred and twenty nine men from this one community were lost in a freak storm. Many of the six-man boats tried to get back to harbour but the gale swept them onto the rocks in the bay and women and children had to watch their menfolk drown.

I loved writing this play. It was as though Jean, Molly and Janet simply walked into the room and sat down with me. I hope it will go some way towards preserving the detail of the lives of nineteenth century herring lassies and fish wives. They deserve to be remembered.

Safe was written as a personal response to the safety-versus-freedom debate – a fraught issue for parents in the twenty-first century. We have to balance this equation every day of our children's lives and it is increasingly hard to keep that balance when our screens and newspapers seem to be full of stories of murdered children. We become easy targets for sensationalist reporting and our sense of stranger-danger is blown up out of all proportion to the actual risk. Vigilante parents, armed with nothing more substantial than gossip, march against suspected paedophiles and our children's freedom to play is eroded as we try to keep them safe from the monsters 'out there'. This is not a new fear. The monsters have always been with us and we have always tried to keep our children safe – after all, what are fairytales but warnings to stay on the path and avoid strangers? But monsters are shape-shifters. They are not always 'out there'. In fact, the statistics show that monsters are usually much closer to home. The numbers of children harmed or killed by strangers are tiny compared with the numbers harmed or killed by other family members or someone they know.

In *Safe*, five parents turn up at an old recycling warehouse to build a fairytale float for the carnival. As night closes in, the twenty-first century becomes Once-Upon-A-Time and the monsters begin to stir in the shadows of the warehouse. The five find themselves increasingly caught up in the imagery and symbolism of fairytales – and, more particularly, in the story of Hansel and Gretel – as they each face up to the dilemmas of modern parenting and the failings of their own mothers and fathers.

The play is full of fairy tale conventions – keys and locked doors, clocks and time, hidden middle names which, when discovered, give power over the owner – and, of course, transformation. Each of the five parents has an alter-ego within the Hansel and Gretel story. The witch is Lilith's alter-ego. Her name means 'of the night'. Lilith is also the name of a female Assyrian demon – a much earlier form of the witch-figure in Hansel and Gretel. Like all female demons and ogres she is incomplete and craves other people's children. Ursula's name means little bear. Gretel is her alter ego, the girl whose father 'lost' her in the forest. Julie corresponds to the mother in the fairytale. She loves her son but has had to raise him by herself and sometimes sees him as a changeling child. She has guilty fantasies of abandoning him on a rich couple's doorstep – a 'safe' version of the old practice of exposing unwanted children. Tim Forester is the father figure, forced by his wife to abandon his daughter. Peter is Hansel, abandoned by his mother and, consequently, a lost boy ever after.

And then there are the wasteground scenes – the third strand of the play and a vulgar, funny reminder that however anxious we become, our children will always be out there, stronger than we think, wiser than we fear – simply getting on with the business of living.

Devil's Ground was a joint commission with NTC Touring Theatre Company and the Borders Festival. My brief was to write a play about the reivers, a group of robbers and bandits who lived in the Scottish Borders at a time when the area was a violent and lawless place. We sometimes tend to bathe the past in a romantic light, but there was nothing romantic about the reivers. Each family ruled their patch by means of intimidation and violence in the same way that gangs rule on 'no-go' housing estates today. They were violent men who made a living from robbery, cattle rustling, blackmail and murder, but there was great family loyalty too. In parallel with the Mafia families of today, the honour of the reiver family Name was of the utmost importance. There were many feuds and a complex system of compensation and retribution was in place. The reivers were tolerated by the authorities of the time because they policed the border and brought rough order of a sort to an otherwise lawless place.

The play is set at the end of the sixteenth century, a time when the unification of the English and Scottish crowns under James I was imminent. This was a watershed time for the reivers. In the new, unified Britain, their brave and violent nature suddenly made them dangerous liabilities. Their end was coming and they knew it, but their pride would not let them change. Within a few years, James had wiped out the reiver families in a systematic act of genocide.

I chose to tell the bigger story of the end of the reivers through the personal drama of one family in crisis. I placed the action of the play within the defensive pele tower in order to echo the sense of claustrophobia the reivers must have felt as the authorities closed in. More than anything else, this play is an exploration of what happens to a family when they are left with no option but to stand and face their own destruction.

Ann Coburn

Acknowledgements

Get Up And Tie Your Fingers

For the first production: thanks to Hazel Wager for making the play happen and for her tireless enthusiasm; Laurence Payne for his sensitive direction; Alison Coates, Lyndsey Maples and Wendy Summers of Fourth Wall Productions – three actors who stepped into my characters as though they had always known them and who also showed they had nerves of steel when they took the play so far on so little funding; Liz Smith and Jonathan Stone for smoothing the way; Howard Craggs, Joy Mitchell, Joe Kerr, Graham Cumming and Judith Payne for giving so freely of their time, facilities or expertise. Subsequent productions: thanks to Gillian Hambleton, director of N.T.C. Touring Theatre Company, for helping me to develop the play further and for the wonderful combination of passion and practicality she brings to every production; Cath Young for an inspirational set; Jo-Anne Horan, for a fresh, intuitive and very astute eye; Janine Birkett, Lindsay Bruce Sharp, Karen Traynor and Gillian Hambleton for finding the truth and for making all those people cry; Priscilla Day, Andy Ross and Richard Stadius for wardrobe, set and stage management; Hilary Burns, Anna Flood and Susan Young for just about everything else.

Safe

Thanks to Gillian Hambleton for understanding absolutely everything and for her creativity as a director; Cath Young for opening all those doors once again; Janine Birkett, Alison Coates, Jo-Anne Horan, Stewart Howson and Peter G. Reed for their generous help with ideas; Nicola Berry, Andy Crawford, Jane Dixon, Peter G. Reed and Karen Traynor for more than fulfilling my expectations and for giving the piece such energy and life; Craig Davidson for his unflappable stage management; Trish Havery, Ian Patience and Andy Ross for wardrobe, scene painting and set building; Hilary Burns, Anna Flood and Susan Young for just about everything else – again.

Thanks also to Nicki Stoddart for all her support.

GET UP AND TIE YOUR FINGERS

Characters

JEAN

a woman in her late thirties or
early forties. Molly's mother

MOLLY

a girl of fifteen. Jean's daughter

JANET

Jean's friend. A widow with three sons

The play can be adapted to suit any staging.

Get Up And Tie Your Fingers was first performed in Eyemouth on 14 October 1995, and throughout the Scottish Borders, by Fourth Wall Productions as part of the Borders Festival, with the following cast:

JEAN, Lyndsay Maples

MOLLY, Wendy Summers

JANET, Alison Coates

Director, Laurence Payne

ACT ONE

SECTION ONE – MAY

*A raised square stage with a wooden pole rising, mast-like, from
one of the back corners. The pole has a small shelf nailed to it, at
slightly above head height, echoing a crow's nest. The shelf has
a rail around it like a galley shelf on a boat. There is a larger
shelf at chest height with a metal hook on a short chain hanging
beneath. Behind the stage, three nets are hung from ceiling to floor.
A narrow gang-plank projects from the middle of the front edge
of the raised stage. Three large wooden barrels stand on the floor,
one in each back corner, one in a front corner.*

*Debris is scattered across the raised stage, reminiscent of the
aftermath of a shipwreck. Three or four battered wooden boxes,
overturned – three nets draped over them – and a scattering of
bleached sticks.*

Scene 1

*The sound of waves breaking on a shore starts the scene. JEAN,
JANET and MOLLY walk in line to stand behind the three nets.
They are all dressed in a similar fashion. Lace up boots, a blouse
with the sleeves rolled up and a long skirt ending just above the
ankles. JEAN carries a large lidded box or basket (a kist) with a
shoulder strap. MOLLY carries a skep (oval tray-like basket for
holding coiled, baited lines) and JANET a wooden bucket. A pause,
then the lights brighten as they move out onto the floor. They sing
a haunting, three part harmony – an old Gaelic seal calling song
or similar. They stop to survey the wreckage – a beat – then move
on, still singing. JEAN moves onto the raised stage and places her
kist in one of the front corners. She begins to turn the wreckage
into a home, while the other two remain on the floor. The sticks
become a pile of kindling, the nets are thrown off onto the floor.
A kettle is hung from the metal hook, a rack of pipes put on the
lower shelf, a pair of large, highly prized matching shells placed*

on the higher shelf with great care (all retrieved from the boxes).
The song ends.

JANET: (*To audience.*) Listen. (*JANET pauses, relishing the sudden silence, allowing it to stretch.*) Quiet, isn't it?
(*JEAN and MOLLY position themselves on the floor space so that each stands beside a different section of the audience. Unlike JANET, they are not communicating with the audience, but looking beyond them – out to sea, searching for something. Each woman acts as though she is alone.*)
That's a waiting quiet, that is. Aye, we're all waiting and watching, every last one of us. Spring is tipping over into summer and the herring should be here.

MOLLY: (*Dreamily, still searching the sea.*) The silver darlings. (*Makes a darting, fishlike movement with her hand.*) Quicksilver – !

JEAN: (*Anxious, searching.*) Forked tail. Silvery white belly

MOLLY: (*Lifting her arms and her face.*) – to match the sky –

JEAN: – and blue green back –

MOLLY: (*Looking downwards.*) – to match the sea –
(*JEAN and MOLLY resume their searching. JANET lifts her head and resumes her conversation with the audience.*)

JANET: My three boys are down at the harbour with the rest of the menfolk, tending boats that were set a week ago and checking nets already mended. (*She smiles and leans forward confidentially.*) Men like to look busy when they're idle. They make work out of nothing to hide the waiting, for fear they shall turn their luck, but waiting is what they're doing. Waiting and fretting that the silver darlings might swim in different waters this season, and take our living with them.

JEAN: – How to find them? Watch for diving gannets –

MOLLY: – moonlight pulls them –

JEAN: – a herring shoal can turn the sea milk white –

MOLLY: – or blood red –

JEAN: – follow the smell of them, oily, rich, rising out of the water –
(*JANET, JEAN and MOLLY all take a deep breath. JANET breathes out again, smiling.*)

JANET: Mmmm. Fresh air… I'd best enjoy it while I can, for soon this whole place will only smell of one thing – herring guts. Aye, we'll be up to our necks in the silver darlings, God willing.

(*MOLLY begins to 'la' the tune of 'Ballerma', the children's hymn – a girl enjoying the sunshine with nothing much on her mind. At the same time, JEAN hurries to the floor space at the back of the stage, strings up a washing line and hangs out some white sheets. JANET cocks her head at the sound of MOLLY's tune. Still talking to the audience.*) That's Molly, Jean's lass, dreaming along the quayside and keeping out of her mam's way. Jean'll be the only one indoors today, I'll warrant. Cleaning. She cleans her house every day except the Lord's Day. Aye, Sundays put Jean in a fair rage of a temper. It eats away at her, having to sit quiet and Christian and watch the dust specks gathering, so she cleans twice as hard on a Monday, to make up. In all the years I've lived here, I've never once seen her at the Thursday June Fair. The whole town goes to the fair, but not Jean. She has to clean her house. She'd climb right out of the coffin and clean up at her own funeral, that one. (*She stands and picks up her bucket. She pauses, thinking.*) I'd dearly love to know what drives her so.

(*JANET moves to the edge of the floor space and sits, as JEAN moves onto the raised stage and begins to scrub the floor.*)

Scene 2

In the cottage, JEAN stops her work as MOLLY enters, still singing. MOLLY stops singing, steps carefully over the clean floor and leans her skep against the boxes. Throughout the next few exchanges JEAN stows the bucket and scrubbing brush and arranges the boxes to make a table and chairs. She places MOLLY's skep on top of the table, takes a lace cloth from one of the boxes and spreads it over the skep to serve as a table cloth.

JEAN: Singing again, is it? Singing willnae buy food or clothes, lass. Where've you been all morning?

MOLLY: Watching for the fleet.

JEAN: Watching for – what am I to do with you, Molly? We are all watching for the fleet, but we work too, lass. We work! I've been scrubbing that floor all on my own without my daughter to lend a hand.

MOLLY: Mam, I scrubbed the floor with you yesterday. We were on our hands and knees half the morning. It must be the cleanest floor in the whole town –

JEAN: Don't you tell me what's clean! I know what's needed better than a slip of a girl…

(MOLLY turns away. JEAN controls her temper with an effort.)

So – where did you go? Up on the cliffs?

MOLLY: No.

JEAN: Where then?

MOLLY: I was down in the harbour with Da and Billie, but all they could speak of was the news Rolling Jack brought.

JEAN: What news?

MOLLY: Rolling Jack says the fleet netted enough herring to keep the gutters up the coast working all night last week. Our Billie was pleased to hear about the big catches but Da was worriting over whether there'd be enough left for us. They've been arguing it out all morning, Da and Billie – round and round, like lobsters in a bucket. So, do you know what I did? I went along to the curing yards and I spied on old Sinclair –

JEAN: Mr Sinclair to you.

MOLLY: – and he was running between the barrels and the salt piles like a wee clockwork mannikin. Salt…barrels… salt…barrels…

(As MOLLY talks, she mimics his worried pacing and JEAN laughs despite herself, a short, hard laugh, quickly over with. Encouraged, MOLLY elaborates the story and the mimicry.)

He kept pulling out his gold watch and frowning at it, as if the herring had promised they'd be on the morning train. Oh, mam, he was in such a taking!

JEAN: Aye, the waiting always makes him fret.

MOLLY: His fingers were jumping and hopping, adding up all the money he's paid out in hiring fees and not one pickled herring to show for it yet.

(*MOLLY laughs again but JEAN does not join in this time.*)

JEAN: And this season you're one of the lassies with his coins in your pocket. He hired you on my word that you'd be a good, fast gutter so, come on now. You've got some practising to do.

(*JEAN fetches a pile of white cotton bandage strips from the kist and dumps them on the table. MOLLY, meanwhile, tiptoes towards the door.*)

(*Calmly, without looking up.*) Molly? Don't even think about it.

(*MOLLY unwillingly turns back.*)

Right, let's see you tie your fingers.

(*MOLLY approaches the table, every inch of her showing her reluctance, and begins to wrap her fingers in the bandage strips.*)

No, no, no! Far too slow. You've to wrap them quick and tie them tight.

MOLLY: Oh, I cannae do it! Why do I have to practise, mam? Why cannae you or Janet tie them for me?

JEAN: We willnae have the time once the season is upon us. When the fleet comes in at dawn with enough herring to fill up the harbour, me and Janet'll be too busy getting ourselves ready.

MOLLY: – Oh, to fill up the harbour…

JEAN: Aye, and Mr Sinclair'll send the caller to rouse us from our beds –

(*MOLLY interrupts, imitating the sing-sing voice of the caller.*)

MOLLY: Get up and tie your fingers!

JEAN: – for he'll want it gutted, salted, sorted and into barrels while it's still fresh enough to wink an eye at you. Now, Molly, as soon as you hear the caller, you've to get down to the curing yards, otherwise me and Janet'll be gutting without a packer, do you see?

MOLLY: But enough herring to fill the harbour! Think how many that is.

JEAN: Molly! Forget the fish. I'm trying to tell you you're part of a crew now. You need to be speedy! Can you do that?

MOLLY: Yes, mam.

JEAN: Let's see you, then.

(*MOLLY picks up the first bandage strip again and wraps it around her finger. JEAN stands, arms folded, watching her and soon MOLLY begins to fumble. She finishes wrapping the first finger and attempts to tie a knot.*)

No, no, no! What did I tell you? Use your teeth. To tie the knot!

(*MOLLY does so, clumsily, and becoming increasingly distressed by her mother's critical attention.*)

Oh, see? See? Why, your Da was a fool to let you stay on at school! Three pennies a week we've had to pay. Three pennies! And for what?

(*MOLLY silently mouths 'Three pennies a week' in unison with JEAN while her back is turned.*)

MOLLY: – Spinning globes – shiny maps – the Empire painted red –

JEAN: – I told him it was a waste of money and good working years. It's too late to teach a great lump of a girl like you. You're nearly a woman, so you are! Ach, your Da is as soft as river mud over you.

MOLLY: (*Ripping off the bandage strips.*) My Da is not soft!

JEAN: You two. All right. (*She places three baskets and a pile of kindling on or beside the table.*) Prove it. Show me all that extra schooling has not ruined you for work.

MOLLY: Yes, mam.

JEAN: Now, you've seen the lassies working down in the yards. Did you mind how they sorted the herring into sizes as they gutted, ready for the barrels?

MOLLY: Yes, mam.

JEAN: (*She points to the baskets.*) These are herring barrels, and… (*She points to the kindling.*) …these are herring.

(*MOLLY giggles. JEAN rounds on her.*)

Oh, what is it now, you flighty wee thing?

MOLLY: Mam. Those herring'll not pass the fisheries inspector.

JEAN: Molly!

MOLLY: Where are they bound, mam? Where will the barrels go?

JEAN: Russia. Now –

MOLLY: Russia! They have palaces and churches there with roofs made of gold and shaped like turnips. Think of that, mam! All those golden 'neeps shining in the sun. Oh, I'd like to see that –

JEAN: Molly! Size them. Call them as you sort.

(*Sighing, MOLLY selects pieces of kindling and throws them into one of the three baskets, according to their size.*)

MOLLY: That's a Mattie, that's a Full, that's a half-full, that's another Mattie – Ow! And that's a splinter.

JEAN: Now, see. That's why you need to tie your fingers… If that'd been your gutting knife, you'd be cut to the bone now and no use to anyone. A deep wound with the salt in it won't mend in a hurry… (*She bends over MOLLY's hand and removes the splinter but then, in a rare moment of tenderness, she does not let go. Instead, she strokes her daughter's fingers.*) Soft hands, see. They'll toughen up, right enough.

MOLLY: (*Turning their hands over to look at JEAN's palms.*) Oh, mam. Look at the scars on your poor hands, all purple and swollen…

JEAN: Don't feel sorry for me, lass. Proud of these hands, I am. They show how hard I work.

(*MOLLY is made brave by her mother's rare gentleness.*)

MOLLY: Mam? I – I – When I dwell on what it means to be a fishwife, with a man and his bairns all looking to me for food and care, and the work… Oh, mam, I get such a tightening here – (*She presses their clasped hands to her breastbone.*) – as though the air has clotted up inside me. It hurts, mam. It feels like drowning…

JEAN: Whisht, child. You mustnae fret so. Every fisher lassie doubts herself when she sees the work ahead. But they all learn to manage, for they come from good, strong stock. Aye, they are bred to it. Besides, no young fishwife is ever alone – do y'ken? And, Molly lass, don't pay any mind to my blethering. You could do the work, if you would only put your heart into it.

MOLLY: No, mam, no! I cannae put my heart into it, for I don't want it. I don't want the gutting and the bait gathering and never the time to lift my head and look about me.

When I think of marrying Angus and living out my whole life here, I – (*She bangs her clasped hands against her breastbone in an attempt to demonstrate her feelings of suffocation.*) Mam… I want to see further than our harbour wall.

JEAN: Well! Then you are a silly, wicked girl!

MOLLY: Mam –

JEAN: We are needed here, Molly. No man could be a fisher without a wife! Remember that. And don't you be so quick to turn your nose up at Janet's boy. You are lucky any lad wants to wed you, the way you drift aboot.

MOLLY: Mam, I like Angus fine! But… I don't know if I love him –

JEAN: Love? You want love, too? Now, you listen to me, Mollie. This is the life you were born to. You cannae throw it off like an old shawl. What else could you turn to?

MOLLY: (*Frightened by her mother's anger, but still trying to make her point.*) Mam, I – I thought, if the minister would write me a letter, I could go to work for a Lady. They have grand houses in Edinburgh, mam, and in London – even over the sea…a – and sometimes, when they travel, they take their best maids with them –

JEAN: Hah! So, you think if you curtsey prettily enough, you'll catch your Lady's eye and she'll up and take you jaunting alongside her?

MOLLY: Aye, I do. Oh, mam, I'd look after her so well she'd have to take me, for she'd not manage without me.

JEAN: You wee fool! Your Lady'd never set eyes on you for you'd never leave the kitchen. You'd be set on as a scullery maid, just like poor, wee Annie Dougal. I'll give you seeing further! How far is Annie seeing now, in her little wooden box in the kirkyard?

MOLLY: But, mam –

JEAN: Mollie, no lass of mine is going into service and there's an end to it!

MOLLY: Then I shall do nothing. My Da will keep me out of the yards if I ask him to. I know he will.

JEAN: Your Da will do no such thing!

MOLLY: *My* Da willnae make me do something I hate.

He loves me. (*She pauses, then repeats the phrase more deliberately.*) He loves *me*.

(*Infuriated, JEAN slaps MOLLY across the face. MOLLY claps her hand to her cheek. They stand glaring at one another, breathing hard then MOLLY turns her back.*)

Scene 3

Suddenly JANET rushes in, excited and out of breath.

JANET: The herring fleet's sighted! Rolling Jack spied it through his glass. I came straight to tell you, as soon as the call went up… (*She comes to a halt and takes in the scene in front of her.*) Aye, I thought that would excite you.

(*JANET looks from one to the other with a wearily amused expression. She has witnessed similar stand-offs many times before.*)

Molly, there's a bucket full of water standing half way down the lane. Go and fetch it, lass. Hurry, now!

(*MOLLY turns to the door. With a glance behind to make sure her mother is not looking, MOLLY reaches up to the paired shells and quickly grabs one, slamming it onto the lower shelf. JEAN sees what MOLLY has done. With a cry of rage, she rushes at MOLLY, who makes a smart exit.*)

JEAN: Oh, what am I to do with her?

JANET: Come and sit down and tell me all about it.

(*JANET indicates a chair and stands waiting. JEAN veers towards it, then heads off to replace the shell (exact alignment). Satisfied, she heads back to the chair, nearly sits down, then jumps up again. JANET looks down at the chair then back to JEAN.*)

JEAN: Janet, I'm awful sorry.

JANET: Here, sit down and tell me why you're sorry.

(*JEAN again nearly sits down, then springs up again. JANET shrugs her shoulders and sits down herself.*)

JEAN: I'm sorry because the herring draive is upon us and we do not have a good crew, Janet. I cannae get the child to work. She says – (*Her voice rises in astonishment.*) – she says she doesnae want to work. Have you ever heard such a thing?

(JANET begins to laugh and then to laugh even more at the outraged expression on JEAN's face.)

I tell you I have a lass who willnae work and you laugh?

(JANET tries to say something, but dissolves once again into hoots of laughter before getting herself under control.)

JANET: Oh, Jean. Don't look at me like that, or I shall never stop.

JEAN: Fools! I am ringed about with fools!

JANET: Aye, well, you must be right there, Jean. We must all be fools, for none of us can fathom how to stop peeving you.

JEAN: You'll be peeved too, when we cannae earn a decent wage this summer.

(JANET stands and moves around the table, surveying the wood and the baskets set out for the practice session.)

JANET: I don't know Jean, maybe the lass has turned against all your drilling. *(She lifts a piece of kindling and lets it fall.)* I'm sure she'll come up to speed when she's caught up in the rush of the work…

(JEAN moves in and tidies away the kindling and bandage strips.)

JEAN: Am I to give in to her every time she finds a thing wearisome? How is she to learn except by drilling? Anyway, there's more than boredom talking in the lass. Molly stood right here and told me she didnae want to be a fishwife. She has a notion to travel. As a Lady's maid…

JANET: Ah, now we get to the heart of it. I see what Molly needs. She has to have a reason for working.

JEAN: Ach! Is putting food into her mouth and clothes on her back not a reason? That's good enough for all the other lassies –

JANET: Whisht Jean! Does the reason matter as long as the work is done? Leave Molly to me. I think I know how to get her into the yards.

(JEAN begins a retort but stops when MOLLY enters and dumps JANET's bucket at the door. MOLLY will not look at JEAN.)

Scene 4

MOLLY: There you are, Janet. I didnae spill a drop. I'm away
　　to see the fleet come in…

*(MOLLY turns and is about to run out again, but JANET
stops her.)*

JANET: Nay, lass, come back. There'll be nothing for you to
　　see yet, even with your sharp eyes – the boats are many
　　miles off, and they must wait for the tide to turn before
　　they can come into harbour.

*(MOLLY turns and drags back into the room. MOLLY and
JEAN make a point of ignoring one another.)*

　　Well now. And what shall we talk about? What's that you
　　say? You want to hear more news of the fleet our men will
　　be joining this very night? Well, Rolling Jack says it is one
　　of the biggest he has known.

JEAN: A big fleet? Now that is a good sign.

JANET: He was sober too, mind, when I met him – walking
　　as steady as the minister. And he claims he saw a storm of
　　gulls above the boats –

JEAN: Oh, there must be herring aplenty for the gulls to fol-
　　low so!

JANET: Aye. We may be in for a rich harvest this season, God
　　willing.

*(She slides a sideways glance at MOLLY and sees that she
is beginning to take an interest.)*

　　Molly here will soon walk right across the harbour at high
　　tide, without once getting her feet wet.

MOLLY: And how would I do that? Even at the lowest tide,
　　the river still runs mid-channel.

JANET: Ah, but the fleet Rolling Jack spied will fill our
　　harbour. There'll be so many boats packed together, you'll
　　jump from deck to deck all the way across.

*(MOLLY begins to be caught up in the exciting picture
JANET is creating.)*

JEAN: Jumping decks? No lass of mine is going to do such a
　　thing –

JANET: Jean –

JEAN: – skirts flying and stockings showing for all to see! And
　　the danger!

JANET: – Jean –

JEAN: – One slip and your leg would be caught between the boats –

JANET: Jean! You can take from my bucket. For your kettle. To make some tea.

(*JANET smiles at JEAN. JEAN glares.*)

JEAN: And just what sort of a house do you think I keep here? My kettle is never empty. Never.

(*JEAN goes to the kettle to make tea. JANET turns to MOLLY.*)

JANET: And the harbour willnae be the only place bursting at the seams. Every spare room in the town will be packed full of –

MOLLY: – herring lassies!

JANET: Aye. We'll go to meet them from the train tonight, shall we?

MOLLY: Oh, yes please!

JANET: You too, Jean, if you'd like.

JEAN: I have better things to fill my time.

JANET: Ach, Jean, one of these years I shall drag you to that train. You are missing such a sight! All those lassies pouring from the carriages and marching through the streets to their lodgings –

MOLLY: With their kists and their Sunday hat boxes –

JANET: Oh, it's a grand sight. And the noise!

MOLLY: You should hear it, mam –

JEAN: Ach, I can hear it fine as they tramp past my window.

MOLLY: All the singing and the shouting –

JANET: – and their great, heavy boots racketing down the road…

(*JANET begins to stamp her feet to the beat of the song 'Herring Lassies'. MOLLY joins in but JEAN will not be tempted. JANET and MOLLY sing a chorus of the song, stamping their feet and reeling. JEAN walks off to the washing line at the back of the stage and takes down a couple of the sheets, leaving the largest sheet in the centre of the line. She brings the washing basket back onto the raised stage. There should be a 'sheet' made of parachute silk already hidden in the basket.*)

Aye, they're a lively lot, all right. It makes me wish

I was still one of them, travelling the herring from Wick
down to Yarmouth.

MOLLY: Tell me, Janet.

JANET: Again?

MOLLY: Aye. Please, Janet. Every spring the three of you
packed your kists…

JANET: …and followed the herring down the coast. There
was me, my sister Katherine and my cousin Mary. We
made a grand crew, so we did. Our fingers fairly flew. Fifty
herring a minute was our Katherine's gutting record, and
Mary, she could pack them so tight, the little darlings had
no need of a barrel round them after a week of pickling.
They could stand there all on their own.

JEAN: Ach! Such tales!

JANET: I'm telling you true! They tried it once, in Peter-
head, when the inspector was after checking the herring
before he would brand the barrels. The cooper knocked
the hoops off one of our Mary's barrels and opened up
the staves like a daisy – and those herring did not move
an inch.

JANET/MOLLY: (*In well rehearsed unison; this tale has been told
many times.*) Not one inch!

JANET: They kept the shape of the barrel down to the last
curve. Aye, the curer was right pleased. He gave the
cooper such a time after that, saying he had no need of
new barrels with our Mary packing for him – he could
send the fish off on their own and use the old barrels again.
That cooper married our Mary, so he did.

JANET/MOLLY: He had to!

JANET: Before she put him out of a job!

> (*JANET's laugh is infectious. Even JEAN joins in and the
> tension between JEAN and MOLLY is finally dissipated.
> JEAN stands behind JANET's chair and starts to fold the
> washing from the basket. MOLLY moves to help JEAN.*)
And the things you see, lass, travelling the herring. One
night, up at the top of Scotland, when we were gutting late,
I saw…

MOLLY: What?

JANET: It was an awful cold night. My feet were in three pairs
of socks inside my boots and still they were froze. And
my hands! As blue as gull's eggs. I had my head down,
gutting away, when I heard Katherine beside me give a
wee squeak. I looked across thinking she had cut herself.
Katherine was standing there, up to her elbows in fish guts,
staring at the sky. So, I looked up too.

MOLLY: What? What did you see?

JANET: Now, the sky was clear, not a wisp of cloud, and, do
you know, it was full of colours!

MOLLY: Colours?

(*JEAN and MOLLY have been folding washing throughout
this story. As JANET goes on to describe the aurora and
they are both caught up, they pick up the parachute silk
sheet, shake it out and throw it up, holding onto the corners.
There are the colours, dancing on the sheet they hold and
moving across the sheet still on the line.*)

JANET: Aye. Great big ribbons of pink and green and purple
and gold, dancing across the sky, all shimmering and
bright! My, it was a grand sight. I could hear them too, so
I could. They made a shivering, tinkling sound, as if they
had hundreds of wee bells caught up in them. (*She is silent
for a moment, remembering.*) They stayed with us all night.

MOLLY: (*Enchanted.*) Oh, Janet…

(*JEAN comes back to herself, gives a disdainful sniff and
swiftly folds the sheet away. The colours disappear.*)

JANET: Aye, it was one of the most beautiful sights on God's
earth and I have never forgotten it.

MOLLY: Now the trains, Janet. Let's do the trains.

(*As she talks, MOLLY arranges the boxes to make a seat in
a train carriage. JANET sits down. As she starts the next
speech, MOLLY makes a pantomime of pulling down the
window and waving as the train pulls out.*)

JANET: When the fleet followed the herring down the coast,
we would follow them, see. We'd all pile in to the one wee
train carriage together, us and a second crew we always
travelled with.

MOLLY: (*Cheekily.*) Bye, mam!

(*MOLLY closes the carriage window and sits down next
to JANET.*)

JANET: Mary would get the stove out to make tea and we'd all take our boots off and get comfy.

(*MOLLY starts to remove her boots.*)

JEAN: Molly…

(*MOLLY makes a face and contents herself with relaxing into a very ungainly position.*)

JANET: There was a ripe smell, I can tell you, what with the heat and the steam –

JEAN: Oh, I'd be shamed! Now, where's the harm in washing your stockings once in a while?

JANET: By the end of the season, we'd travelled all the way down to Yarmouth.

(*MOLLY suddenly jumps from her seat and stands front stage, grinning at JANET.*)

MOLLY: Watch, Janet. Who am I?

(*MOLLY puts on an exaggeratedly haughty walk, nose in the air, ladylike steps, hands held limply at chest level. JANET laughs.*)

JEAN: Ach, that poor lassie…

JANET: Poor! That she was not, with her hands as white and soft as a pair of Eyemouth haddocks and never a day's work done in her life!

JEAN: You know fine what I mean by poor. What you lassies did to her…

JANET: (*Chuckling.*) Aye, she didnae look so grand when we'd finished –

MOLLY: Stop! You've to tell it right, Janet. Start with the ladies and gentlemen.

JANET: Aye, well down at Yarmouth you get a lot of fine gentlefolk coming to the quays. They travel from London for the sea air and then they stroll aboot, trying to find something to fill their time, and some of them stop to watch the work. Now, we didnae mind the ones who came to marvel at the skill and the speed of it, but there were some who came to put on airs, see, with us all covered in fish muck and them in their fine silks and best button boots. There was a lassie there one season. She was down at the quays every day, standing as close as she dared, the better to show her white skin and her tiny waist next to us – and the things she'd say!

MOLLY: (*She resumes her exaggerated pose and puts on her idea of an upper class accent.*) Oh, have you ever seen such creatures? And how they do smell! (*She presses an imaginary handkerchief to her nose.*) I truly cannot bear it.

JANET: There! You have her! After a week we'd had our fill. We took our chance, me and Katherine. We marched up behind her and emptied our gut tub over her head!

(*JANET mimes the action and MOLLY reacts.*)

It was full, mind, and some of those guts had been standing in the sun for a good while.

(*JANET begins to laugh, remembering, and MOLLY joins in.*)

The brim of her wee hat was – was swimming…a – and her dress…

(*JANET stops, she is laughing too much to talk. JEAN keeps a straight face until JANET and MOLLY eventually stop laughing. Then, to their surprise, JEAN bursts out laughing and sets them off again.*)

JEAN: You were foolish. What if you had been caught?

JANET: Nay, by the time she scraped the guts from her face, we were back at the farlanes with all the other lassies. She couldnae get away fast enough. That was the last of her. Mind, if she thought we looked bad in the daytime, it's as well she never saw us on the nights we had to work through.

The singing was the only thing that kept us going. Aye, rhythm for our fingers and tunes to keep us lively.

(*MOLLY begins to sing 'The Song of the Fish Gutters'. JANET, then JEAN join in. All three women sing the song, a spirited rendition.*)

MOLLY: I'd love to travel the herring. It'd be grand.

JANET: And what is stopping you?

MOLLY: I have no one to crew with.

JANET: Maybe not this season, but there are three lassies from my home village arriving on the train tonight. They'll be lodging with me. Now, I've heard they'll be needing a third next season, for Fiona's getting wed at the end of this one. So, Molly, if you can come up to speed and impress them, I'll put in a word for you.

(*Neither MOLLY nor JANET have looked at JEAN dur-*)

ing this last speech. They have not noticed her increasingly anxious expression.)

MOLLY: Oh, mam, wouldnae that be grand? To see all those places…
(*At this, JEAN jumps up and grabs the mug from JANET's hand just as she is about to take a gulp.*)

JEAN: (*To MOLLY.*) You and your travelling! Curing yards – that's all you'd see – and the inside of a herring looks the same wherever you gut it.
(*JEAN takes MOLLY's mug from her too, rushes them away and begins to clear up the kindling and baskets. MOLLY looks at JANET anxiously, but JANET pats her hand and makes a reassuring face.*)

JANET: Molly, be a good lass and take my water bucket home for me.
(*MOLLY exits.*)

Scene 5

JEAN and JANET square up to one another.

JANET: So, Jean –

JEAN: (*Interrupting, hard and angry.*) Whose lass is she?

JANET: Yours, but –

JEAN: But nothing! I'm the one to say what Molly can do, not you! Not you!

JANET: Ach, Jean, I cannae fathom you. You say you want the lass to work. You say you want her to be like all the other lassies –

JEAN: Aye, but not the travelling!

JANET: Why ever not?

JEAN: It isnae safe!

JANET: Safe? Whisht, it is a hard life but no more dangerous than the work she'll be doing here. She will be safe enough.
(*JEAN begins to move around, dusting surfaces, polishing, checking the alignment of the shells etc. Talking distractedly, she lets something slip – a belief which she has never voiced.*)

JEAN: No. I mean she's safe because of me. I've kept my whole family safe these past twenty years, but I cannae keep Molly safe if she moves away…

JANET: You keep them safe? You…?

JEAN: …Aye.

JANET: You mean it…

> (*JEAN will not reply. She picks up MOLLY's shawl and clutches it to her chest.*)

> How? Can you stop the slip of the gutting knife, is that what you are saying? Can you keep the sea calm when the boats are out? Jean, that is a prideful boast. Only God can make such a claim.

JEAN: But that is it! God sees what I do, every day. He sees the payment I make and He keeps them safe, in return.

JANET: Payment! What do you do? How do you pay?

JEAN: I – (*She gestures around the room.*)

JANET: …Ahhh… So, that is what drives you. All those years of scraping up every last speck of dirt. How did it start?

> (*JANET waits but JEAN will not answer.*)

> Will you not tell me? Oh, Jean…this is a cruel God you have.

JEAN: And what of your God, who let your husband drown? Was that not cruel?

JANET: The sea took my man, not God. God gave me strength. He helped me to accept.

JEAN: Ach! Accept, accept! What a weak and sorry word. That is not my way.

JANET: Nor mine. It is a hard task, to accept my man's drowning, not a weakness. I miss him. I grieve for him. I envy you and all women like you, who still have the pleasure of a warm man in their beds –

JEAN: Hush, Janet…

JANET: Why? There is no shame in that. I loved him. I can still remember the smell of his skin…

> (*JEAN gasps and looks away, embarrassed. JANET shakes her head sadly.*)

> I accept things that cannot be helped, Jean. And you – you are wearing yourself out for nothing. You cannae make bargains with God! Molly is no safer here than down in Yarmouth.

JEAN: Aye, well, she'll not be going. No crew will want my dreamy Molly. She'll not get up to speed.

JANET: She might.

JEAN: Not my Molly.

JANET: She might. She has a reason now.

(JANET and JEAN try to stare one another down. Eventually, JEAN yanks off her apron and throws it at JANET.)

JEAN: Well, are we to stand here all day and miss the fleet coming in?

(An exasperated JANET leaves the raised stage and stands next to one of the two barrels which are placed one on each side of the raised stage. MOLLY moves to stand beside the barrel by the gangplank. JEAN stays for a few seconds, pushing in the chairs, swiping a cloth over the range etc. Finally, she picks up MOLLY's shawl, folds it, hugs it to her. She shakes her head.)

Not my Molly.

(JEAN puts MOLLY's shawl away and leaves the raised stage, stopping to straighten up the shells, making sure they are perfectly aligned. She moves to stand by the barrel at the opposite back corner of the stage to JANET.)

Scene 6

A bridging scene between Section One (Spring) and Section Two (Summer).

All three women begin to sing 'The Song of the Fish Gutters'. At the same time, JEAN and JANET roll their barrels to join MOLLY on the floor space at the front of the raised stage. Together they lift the barrels into place on the raised stage to form a triangle, JEAN and JANET's barrels at the two front corners, MOLLY's barrel at the end of the gangplank. They each stand behind their barrels, looking out to sea. MOLLY picks up a pile of three wicker baskets and throws one each to JEAN and JANET, keeping the last one for herself. From the barrels they take rough aprons, strips to tie up the thumbs and first fingers of their left hands and finally gutting knives. The song comes to an end. They hold the knives at the ready. They are nervous, excited, keyed up.

MOLLY: Here they come –

JEAN: The fifies –

JANET: With their red sails snapping –

MOLLY: And their keels so low with the weight of the herring –

JEAN: – it's a wonder they stay afloat!

JANET: Here they come –

MOLLY: Into harbour –

JEAN: Are you ready, lass?

> (*MOLLY nods. A second's pause, then they plunge their hands into the barrels and begin to gut. The following scene should develop a strong beat – plunge, slice, then toss into the baskets behind them. They take up the following chant, one line each.*)

> Mattie…

> Full…

> Half-full…

> Spent…

> (*The chant is repeated several times until the rhythm is established, then one of them moves into the first verse of the song 'Herrin's Heids'. The others join in with the response, keeping up the gutting rhythm. As they reach the first chorus, they pocket the gutting knives, turn, pick up the baskets and toss them to the person on their right, in unison, stopping as the chorus comes to an end and replacing the basket on the floor behind them. Readying their gutting knives, they fall into the gutting rhythm again with the next verse. On the final chorus, MOLLY does not throw her basket, but catches each of the other baskets in her own. They clear the stage of the barrels and baskets, removing aprons and bandage strips as they break up the rhythm of the song, humming snatches of the song to themselves, tired now, winding down. JEAN and MOLLY move off to one side of the space, donning Sunday bonnets and shawls, as JANET turns to talk to the audience.*)

SECTION TWO – AUGUST

Scene 7

JANET: Sunday. We rest, thank The Lord. What a sum-

mer! Herring shoals packed so tight my Angus swears
he could've stepped from the boat and walked to shore
on their backs. (*She chuckles*.) Catches are dwindling now,
mind. The silver darlings are moving too far south for our
boats to reach them. Aye, the season is nearly over for us.
Soon the herring lassies will be moving on.

*(JEAN and MOLLY begin a slow procession around the
floor space, JEAN leading, holding her bible, keeping a
check on MOLLY who is following, full of repressed energy.
JANET notices them and nods towards MOLLY.)*

They asked for Molly this morning, my lodgers. They want
her to crew with them next season. Aye! Dreamy Molly! I
tell you, the lass has amazed us all, the way she's worked.
She found it awful hard at first, but now! Now she's one of
the best gutters I've crewed with, and that's the truth.

*(JEAN and MOLLY have reached the cottage. They remove
their bonnets and shawls. JEAN spreads a lace table cloth
over the table and sits down to read her bible. MOLLY
stares out to sea. JANET lifts a kist and a pair of boots
from the corner of the space and shows the audience.)*

I'm passing these on to the lass. This was my travelling kist
when I was a herring lassie. And these…these were my
man's best sea boots. They willnae fit my boys. Feet as big
as lobster creels, all three of them. He was a wee man. He
always claimed the sea would throw him back
if it ever caught him. But it didnae throw him back. It swallowed him right up. Mind, he had a big heart, for a tiddler.
Maybe the sea knew that. Aye, they'll do fine for Molly, if
the poor lass ever gets away. She talks and talks of travelling the herring and Jean – Ach, Jean! Jean will say nothing,
and the more the lass talks of leaving, the more Jean scrubs.
Three months of gutting and scrubbing – why she's as thin
as a bone and her hands are red raw. Now, what am I to do
for the best?

Scene 8

*JANET shakes her head, then picks up her kist and boots and moves
round to the back of the raised stage. MOLLY, who has grown
increasingly restless, begins to 'tra la' a tune, but is stopped in
mid-note by JEAN.*

JEAN: Hush, lass! (*She indicates upstairs with a jerk of her head.*)
Remember Billy and your Da. They must go out with the
tide at the back of Sunday. They need their sleep.

MOLLY: How can anyone sleep on a day like this? Mam…?
Can I go down to the harbour?

JEAN: That you cannot. You can sit down as it is proper to do
on a Sunday.

MOLLY: Oh, but mam, I sat in the kirk all morning. I shall
burst if I've to sit any more! Can't I go? All the herring
lassies are meeting there –

JEAN: Then they are no better than they should be. Decent lassies dinnae parade around the streets on The Lord's Day.

MOLLY: Parade? Mam, they sit in the sun and knit and tell
stories.

JEAN: Knitting is it? Knitting on a Sunday? Ach, they arnae
decent folk. Mind, if it's stories you're wanting,
I can tell stories, if it will keep you still.
(*Reluctantly, MOLLY sits down opposite her mother. JEAN
begins to tell the story.*)
Now… Let me see… Once there was a feckless lass who
wouldnae settle where she was best off. At home –

MOLLY: Oh, mam – !

JEAN: – at home! Too good to stay with her own folks, this
one. She wanted to be away. Travelling.

MOLLY: Just to see, mam. Just to see…

JEAN: She saw something, right enough.

MOLLY: Something…?

JEAN: She was up on the cliffs watching the fleet put out and
so busy wishing she was with them, she didnae see what
was creeping up behind her.

MOLLY: What?

JEAN: The dark.

MOLLY: Ach. Only the dark?

JEAN: No. Not only. There was something in the dark. Something which kenned what the feckless lass wanted. Something which heard when she swore 'I'd sell my soul to the
Devil if only he would take me travelling – '

MOLLY: She said his name!

JEAN: There came a growl behind her. Oh, what a growl it

38

was! It made her think of grave mud and scrabbling rats. Slowly she turned to look. A great, black dog was sitting there with blazing eyes, gleaming teeth and a pair of horns on its head.

MOLLY: Horns! Oh, mam, that was no dog –

JEAN: Aye, that's what she thought. But here's a strange thing. Her second look showed not horns, but ears. Pointy black ears.

MOLLY: No, no, no! She was right the first time –

JEAN: The feckless lass tried to walk away, but the black dog wouldnae leave her, for she had made the deal. So, she travelled far and wide –

MOLLY: Travelled – !

JEAN: She had tae. She wanted rid of that dog. But it followed her everywhere –

MOLLY: Aye, but – where did she travel?

JEAN: She travelled the whole, wide world and saw…

(*JEAN pauses. MOLLY waits, intent.*)

And saw nothing she couldnae see at home. Houses, folks, streets. All the same.

(*MOLLY stands, turning her back on JEAN.*)

MOLLY: If she thought that, she was no traveller.

JEAN: There were other things on her mind! (*She collects herself and continues.*) Finally, after a year and a day, she came home. Home tae her folks. Home tae her mam.

(*MOLLY reacts with disgust. JEAN continues and MOLLY is drawn back into the tale despite herself. JANET creeps up to the floor area behind the raised stage and listens for a while, as though she is listening at the window. She takes two pegs from the washing line behind her and creeps back to listen again. She is enjoying herself.*)

'I'll keep you safe,' said the mam. But she could do nothing when the black dog came, for the feckless lass had made the deal. First they heard the howling, drifting down from the moors.

'D'ye ken that noise, mam?' said the lass.

'Aye, 'tis only the wind in the chimney.' Next they heard the growling. Oh, it was enough to freeze the blood!

'D'ye ken that noise, mam?' said the lass.

'Aye. 'Tis only the waves beating against the cliffs.' Then came a scritch, scritch, scritch at the door.

'D'ye ken that noise mam?' said the lass.

'Aye. 'Tis only the rats at the tatties' said the mam. 'Now get behind me.' The mam turned to face the door as it *burst open!*

MOLLY: What! What happened!

JEAN: Awful quick it was. The great black dog cracked its jaws apart and swallowed up the lass in one gulp.

MOLLY: And the mam? Did it take her too?

JEAN: (*With a trace of smugness.*) No. Just the lass. She could only sell herself, not her folks, for we are all the keepers of our own souls.

(*At some point in the next speech, JANET discreetly inserts the wooden pegs behind her upper lip so that they look like fangs.*)

You can still hear the black dog sometimes, howling up on the cliffs or growling through the streets looking for another feckless lass to strike a deal with.

(*Behind them, JANET jumps onto the stage with a roar. The result is gratifying. Both JEAN and MOLLY leap from their seats, screaming.*)

Scene 9

JANET doubles up with laughter.

MOLLY: Oh, Janet! You fair frightened the life out of me!

(*They lean together, laughing. JEAN tries to quieten them.*)

JEAN: Hush, now! You'll wake the men.

JANET: Jean, if that yell of yours didnae wake them, nothing will!

JEAN: Was it awful loud?

JANET: Loud? They'll have heard that hoot down at the station!

(*MOLLY doubles up with laughter again. JEAN huffily resumes her seat.*)

JEAN: Ach, away with you!

JANET: Aye, they'll all be rushing onto the platform now, thinking the train's come early.

(*MOLLY and JANET collapse together. JEAN folds her*

arms and turns her back on them. JANET, seeing that JEAN has had enough, sobers up and decides to change the subject.)

My, but you have a way with those stories, Jean. I can see it happening, so I can.

JEAN: (*Pleased, but trying not to show it.*) Aye, well, this one was so restless, I had to do something to keep her quiet.

JANET: She must be picking it up from the fisher lassies. They're flocking in the harbour now, getting ready to head South.

MOLLY: But, have you not asked?

(*JEAN becomes very tense.*)

JANET: No, I didnae ask....

(*JEAN relaxes.*)

MOLLY: But it was agreed! If I came up to speed, you would put in a word for me.

JANET: Molly, I didnae ask them for I didnae need to – they asked me. They want you to crew with them next season, when Fiona's wed.

MOLLY: Oh, Janet, that's grand! That's grand!

JANET: Aye. Now, go and look, in the corner.

(*MOLLY runs over to the kist and sea boots. She does not notice that JEAN and JANET are staring at one another. JEAN is looking at her friend as though she has betrayed her. JANET meets her gaze, sad but determined.*)

They asked *me,* Jean. I am only the messenger.

(*MOLLY comes back, carrying the kist and sea boots.*)

MOLLY: Janet...are these for me?

JANET: Aye, lass.

MOLLY: Thank you, Janet! Look, mam! I have everything I need now.

(*JEAN will not look. MOLLY, pretending that everything is all right, hurries on.*)

I'll run down to the harbour and tell the lassies I'll be glad to crew with them.

(*MOLLY hurries to the door, stops, and looks at JEAN, who has not moved.*)

I'll tell them, then.

(*She waits a few seconds longer, then turns and rushes out.*)

Scene 10

JANET: Jean…? Jean…? Dinnae torment the lass. She's
worked her hands raw this season to catch the eye of those
lassies. I ken how you feel about the lass travelling, but you
cannae stop her now! Give her your blessing, Jean, and let
her go.

(*JEAN will not respond.*)

Aye, well, I shall take that as a yes, since you willnae
answer.

(*JANET waits, but JEAN is still unresponsive. JANET
looks out to sea, still talking to JEAN although her back is
turned. As JANET talks on, unaware, JEAN rises to her
feet, picks up the kist and starts to exit.*)

You'll see. Give the lass a few seasons at the herring and
she'll settle down. Then maybe we'll have a wedding. Her
and my Angus. What do you think?

(*JANET turns in time to see JEAN about to leave the cottage with the kist.*)

Jean…? Jean! Throwing my kist in the harbour willnae
solve a thing.

(*JEAN hesitates then turns and shoves the kist into JA-
NET's arms. JANET puts the kist down and watches
JEAN begin her usual tidying circuit of the room, mak-
ing sure everything is perfect – particularly the shells. As
JEAN moves around, JANET talks to her, but JEAN is
still resolutely silent.*)

There you go again. Round and round, making your pay-
ments to God. What is it? What is this…this black dog
panting at your back and making you so feared?

(*Ignoring JANET, JEAN moves to the mantleshelf and
adjusts the position of the shells again. JANET grabs JEAN
and turns her around.*)

Come out, Jean! I know there is more to you than this!
I see it in your stories –

(*JEAN knocks JANET's hands from her shoulders.*)

JEAN: Stories? I'll give you a story! I'll tell you about a lassie
who lived here in the town. She was a good lassie. She did
as she was told, worked hard and went to the kirk every

Sunday, but that didnae help her when the cholera came. She was thirteen years old. She saw first her wee brother, then her young sister, then her mam fall ill. Have you seen the cholera at work, Janet? It brings a body down in fever and in pain. It drains the life out of them. Do you ken how it was for the lassie, trying to care for her family?

JANET: You know I wasnae living here when the cholera came.

JEAN: No. You werenae. There's an awful, sour stink, Janet. Always and everywhere. For they cannae stop messing themselves. Do you ken how it was for the lassie? Can you see her there, in the heat and the steam and the stink, boiling up the water for the dolly tub to – (*She grabs the three sheets they folded earlier and flings them into the air, one after the other.*) – wash the bedding and wash the bedding and wash the bedding... Can you see her, wiping their bodies clean – (*She bundles a sheet into the shape of a body and uses a corner to tenderly wipe a hidden face.*) – and trying not to breathe too deep for fear she'll catch it too? (*She gently lays the bundle down.*) Can you hear her crying and praying as she runs through the lanes past the barrels of burning tar and down to the well for more and more and more water...? This lassie tried her best. She did. But, one by one, her wee brother – (*She picks up a sheet.*) – and her sister (*And another, tenderly.*) and her mam (*She gathers up the third sheet.*) made the journey from their own beds to the fever hospital in the barracks, then up to their rest in the kirkyard. Soon there was only the lassie and her da.

JANET: Aye. I can see her. The poor, wee lassie. But, Jean, every fish wife in this town lost family to the cholera... Yet they arenae like you –

JEAN: (*Shaking her head vehemently.*) The loss was not all. Not in this story. When the lassie's da fell ill, ach, she was beside herself! She emptied the last coins from her mam's purse and she ran to fetch the doctor.

'Cholera,' he said and the lassie nodded, waiting for him to help her da. But the doctor turned away. 'We're full at the Barracks,' he said. 'You'll have to nurse him here.'

(*JEAN is now so involved in the horror of her story, she stops*

talking about 'the lassie' and slips into a straight account.)
Oh, Janet. I couldnae bear it. Not my da too! I ran after
the doctor and grabbed at his coat tails. Please, Sir, tell me
what to do…! He shook me off his coat like I was a lump
of dirt. He waved his hand around the cottage.
'Look,' he said. I looked and I saw the mess he was seeing
and, oh, Janet, I was shamed.
(*Throughout the next few exchanges, JEAN begins to tidy
up the sheets, as though she is back with the doctor, trying
to put the cottage to rights.*)

JANET: Ach, and what did he expect, with you little more
than a bairn and filling your days with nursing and laun-
dry?

JEAN: 'Clean up your dirt,' he said. 'That's what you can do.
Those who live in filth will catch filthy diseases. You people
can burn as much tar as you like, but you'll not be free of
cholera until you clean up your dirt and boil your drinking
water.'

JANET: I would dearly love to get hold of that doctor.

JEAN: But it worked! I cleaned and polished and tidied until
the whole place was fresh and pure – and my da got better.

JANET: Because you boiled his drinking water! It was the
dirty well water to blame, not your house keeping! Look at
fishy Sam. His place stinks like an unwashed gut barrel, yet
the cholera never touched him. Why? Sam willnae drink
water, only whisky. Ach, Jean, you know we've all been
fine since we had our grand new pump put in…

JEAN: Aye, I know it was the well water. I know it here
(*She points to her head.*) but here… (*She points to her heart.*) …
here I cannae rid myself of what that doctor started.
I clean to keep them safe. They're safe because I clean.
I cannae stop.

JANET: Then let Molly break the circle for you. Let her go.

JEAN: (*Beginning to sob.*) – I – cannae – I

JANET: You are fooling yourself!

JEAN: – cannae – I – cannae –

JANET: You can, Jean. Let her go. Let the Lord watch her for
a while. Let yourself rest!

(JEAN flings herself into JANET's arms and sobs uncontrollably. MOLLY returns. Not knowing what to do, she watches the two of them for a few seconds before JANET looks up and sees her.)

Dinnae fret, lass. Your mam's only sad to see you go.

MOLLY: Mam? Am I to go? Am I to travel the herring?

(JEAN levers herself away from JANET and stands, wiping her face on her sleeve.)

JEAN: *(With a poor attempt at being brisk.)* Whisht, lass, enough of the cow eyed looks. Have you never seen a body greet before?

MOLLY: Not you, mam.

JEAN: Aye, well. If you gawp like that down in Yarmouth, they'll think you're country simple.

MOLLY: Yarmouth? you mean…? *(Flinging herself at JEAN.)* Oh, mam!

(JEAN absorbs MOLLY'S headlong dash, then lifts one hand and, briefly, strokes her daughter's hair. Not wanting to lose control again, JEAN pushes MOLLY away, becoming business-like.)

JEAN: *(To JANET.)* And you can stop grinning like a scarecrow.

(JANET shrugs her shoulders but does not stop grinning.)

(To MOLLY.) Where are they then?

MOLLY: Who?

JEAN: Your lassies. Your crew. Take me to them.

(JEAN pats her hair, smooths down her blouse and skirt and heads for the door.)

MOLLY: *(Following.)* Why, mam?

JEAN: I need to ask them some questions.

MOLLY: What questions?

JEAN: Do they have decent lodgings, do they have Christian habits, do they eat proper meals –

MOLLY: Mam! You cannae –

JEAN: I can and I will! Hurry, now.

(JEAN gestures to MOLLY to go out of the cottage ahead of her. MOLLY exits reluctantly. JEAN follows her, continuing to talk.)

And if you ever shame me by steaming up a train carriage with smelly feet and unwashed stockings…

MOLLY: (*Voice off.*) Oh, mam!

(*JANET remains quite still for a moment, smiling, then she begins to hum and sing snatches of 'Herring's' Heids' whilst giving little hops and jumps. The jigging and the singing slowly grow in pace and volume until she is belting out the chorus and doing an improvised jig around the table. She stops at the end of the chorus, pats her hair, straightens her clothes and exits. All three move to stand behind the nets at the back of the stage.*)

End of Act One.

ACT TWO

SECTION THREE – OCTOBER

Scene 1

JANET, JEAN and MOLLY walk on and once again stand motionless behind the net 'curtain' for a few beats. JANET is carrying her bucket. JEAN and MOLLY both carry the shallow wicker baskets – or skeps – used to gather mussels to bait the lines. The three move out onto the floor. JEAN and MOLLY move one to each side of the raised section and begin to stoop to gather bait. JANET moves up onto the raised stage. Throughout the next speech, the three women keep pausing together, stopping to scan the sky and stare out to sea.

JANET: And what sort of weather is this for the line fishing season? (*Pause – then return to speech/work.*) The past week, we've had wind and rain and seas so rough the boats couldnae leave harbour – yet today… today the sky is as clear and blue as a bairn's eye – and the sea… Look at it! (*Pause – then return to speech/work.*) Not a wave in sight. High summer in October? It's unnatural. The air's so still. When we were out early this morning, gathering bait for the lines, I could hear the women talking across the bay as clear as if they were standing next to me. There was not a breath of wind to fill the sails when the boats went out. The men had to use the oars. Rolling Jack, he… (*Pause – then return to speech/work.*) – Ach well, he warned them not to put out today. He swore he'd never seen the weather glass so low. He said it was the calm before a storm. But what could they do? Were they to sit idle in the sunshine and watch the bait rotting in the barrels? They've been kept ashore the past week with not a penny earned – how could they stay with the sea so milky mild? They had to go… Ach, but I'll be glad to see the boats back in harbour tonight, and that's the truth of it.

(*As JANET picks up her bucket and turns to walk away, the sky darkens. JANET stares out to sea with a horrified expression then exits, running, to the back of the raised stage, as the sound effects for a gale begin to build.*)

Scene 2

The whole of this next scene should be full of restless pacing and movement. The three women should rarely be still, to contrast with the scene after the storm.

JEAN turns and runs to the cottage.

JEAN: Molly? Molly…? (*She rushes to stare out to sea.*) Dear Lord, bring them home. Bring them home! (*She straightens up the shells then grabs a cloth and begins to polish, feverishly.*) (*MOLLY rushes in but JEAN does not stop polishing.*)

MOLLY: Oh, mam, how could a storm move in so fast? It's an awful bad one. What'll we do?

JEAN: Wait. Waiting is all we can do. That's the worst of it.

MOLLY: Mam? Billy and da…will they be – will they…? (*JEAN's face is bleak. She can offer no encouragement.*) My da…

(*JANET enters in a rush. MOLLY runs into her arms. JEAN remains standing stiffly, watching as JANET rocks MOLLY.*)

My da!

JANET: Hush, Molly… Your da is battling to get home to you right now and why should he be doing all the work? You need to get busy, lass. Clean clothes laid out to air, hot water for the tub and a pot of stovies on the range. When they reach harbour, they'll be soaked and frozen and needing food.

MOLLY: You think they'll come home safe?

JANET: Whisht! They are fishers! This coast is in their blood.

MOLLY: But, the waves – the sea is running mountains high!

JANET: Aye, and every crew out there could steer their boat through a whirlpool if they had to. Now, are you going to kill them before their time or make ready for their homecoming?

48

MOLLY: Clothes, water, tatties…and the lamp! The lamp at the window to bring them home!

(*MOLLY rushes off to light the lamp, then continues to work in the background, putting pots and kettles onto the range, taking clothes from a kist etc.*)

JANET: They'll turn up.

JEAN: It's my fault, Janet.

JANET: Ach, Jean –

JEAN: I should have told my man not to go but I said nothing.

JANET: Then we are all to blame. My boys –

JEAN: No. I saw him looking at the skeps with the lines all coiled and ready and I knew what he was thinking. He was thinking all our work would go to waste if they didnae put out. He looked at me and I knew what was in his mind and I said nothing. I was thinking of the waste too, and of them both getting under my feet for another day.

(*JANET rushes to the range and picks up a piece of firewood.*)

JANET: (*Thrusting the stick at JEAN.*) Here. Why don't you beat yourself with it and be done?

(*JEAN knocks the stick away.*)

How much guilt will you try to carry? This is not for your shoulders. The men know the dangers of the fishing. Each time they go out, they risk not coming back.

JEAN: But –

JANET: There were others putting out today, my three boys among them, and your man would have followed them whatever you said.

(*JEAN turns back to her polishing. JANET sighs and turns to MOLLY.*)

Are you done, lass?

MOLLY: Aye, all done. What now?

JANET: Now?

(*JANET looks around the room. For the first time she appears lost. MOLLY runs to JANET.*)

MOLLY: Janet, your boys can make a boat dance through a storm.

JANET: Aye, they'll steer her home, right enough. But those waves could scoop a man from the deck in the blink of an eye.

MOLLY: They'll take care of each other.

JANET: The twins, they work together like one man. I've seen
Robbie throw a line and James catch it without a word or
a glance between them. But Angus now, they'll have to
remember to watch him. And he's just the one to do some-
thing brave and daft. He has no proper fear, my Angus...
(*JEAN comes to comfort JANET too. MOLLY's head
snaps up.*)
MOLLY: Did you hear...? I thought I heard a call...there
again, on the wind...
(*MOLLY rushes to the window and looks out. The others
join her.*)
Look! Something moving on the harbour wall...
JEAN: Crawling into the gale –
JANET: People! They are people. On their hands and knees...
JEAN: (*Grabbing her shawl and tying it around her head.*) They
musthae spotted something.
JANET: (*Running for her shawl, tying it and taking a shawl to
MOLLY.*) Can you see anything else?
MOLLY: – Yes! A boat! The first boat is nearly home!
(*Music – wild, yearning, full of struggle and sadness –
overpowers and replaces the sound of the storm as the women
enact the struggle to reach their men. JANET and JEAN
leave the raised stage and head towards the front of the floor
area as though battling against a gale. MOLLY picks up the
lamp and swings it back and forth in the direction of the sea.
JEAN and JANET each throw a net rope to MOLLY who
attempts to pull it in. Their hands nearly touch but then they
are swept back. The struggle continues until, as the music
becomes calm and sorrowful, the three women become caught
up in the nets, moving like sea weed, like drowned men. The
nets become shrouds, then babes in the women's arms. As the
music fades, the three women drop the nets and slowly return
to the raised stage. MOLLY turns out the lamp.*)

Scene 3

*Quietly, slowly, they each take up their positions. JANET sits at
the end of the ramp. JEAN seats herself beside the lace covered
skep which has been serving as a table. MOLLY picks up a copy*

of the local paper. She steps forward and begins to read. A distant cannon is fired at intervals throughout this speech.

MOLLY: 'The greatest calamity that ever befel the fishing industry of this coast overtook it on Friday the fourteenth of October 1881, when many of our brave fishermen went down to a watery grave. The people, even to the oldest of the inhabitants, agree in saying that the storm was the fiercest they had ever experienced. Its outbreak was so sudden as to give those at sea no opportunity of running for shelter. Many were engaged in hauling in their lines when they were suddenly overtaken by a hurricane, accompanied by torrents of rain. One hundred and twenty nine gallant men were lost, leaving seventy three widows and two hundred and sixty three fatherless children.

'Now, in this once lively community, silence reigns. The galloping horses, drawing carts laden with haddock to the station, have been replaced with slow, rumbling coffin vans. Boats lie idle. A regular percussion disturbs the quiet, as the cannon is fired on the cliff top in an attempt to bring bodies to the surface. Wives and mothers, fathers and brothers, all recount their tales of sorrow. Some are angry and bitter, some outwardly calm, others weep openly, but they all share a need to tell their loss. They all must bear witness.'

(*MOLLY goes to sit at one side of the raised stage.*)

JEAN: Newspapers! There's one paper wanting to give our men medals for their bravery. Medals! Aye, they were brave, right enough, every last one of them, but what good are medals now? And what do they write about us, the women left behind? Do they call us brave and talk of medals? No. We only waited for them to come home. We only watched and searched all these days past. If there were medals for waiting, why we'd be armoured with them. We are dignified, they write. We accept the death of our men. We are not accepting! We choose to keep our sorrow private, with the streets full of strangers come to gawp at us. Some of them tried to follow me this morning. I soon lost them on the cliff path. I couldnae have them gawping at what I had to do. I was searching for my boy. For his body. Do they give medals for searching?

(After this last flash of anger, JEAN settles to telling her story.)
We found the wreck of the boat the day after the storm, but no bodies. Billie he's called. My Billie. My boy.
I named him after my wee brother, William. William died of the Cholera years back. He was a lovely bairn.
(As JEAN talks about her baby boy, she leans forward, smiling, looking into the lace covered skep as though into a crib, rocking the skep gently back and forth.)
When my Billie was born, I thought – I thought God had given me a second chance. There was my brother William, all over again. The same red hair, bright eyes and a smile as slow and sweet as honey. My second chance. And now he is gone.
(JEAN leaves the skep and stands.)
I will find him, though. We thought we had him a few days back. It was a young man's body, the same build as my Billie. Red hair, too. The poor laddie's face was gone, battered by the rocks, but I knew it wasnae my boy as soon as I got close enough to see the pattern on his gaynzey. I made all my Billie's gaynzeys, with my own, special pattern. Good, oiled wool they are, and knitted in the round for strength. The sea shall not tear my gaynzey from his back, however rough it gets. Oh, I want him back! I cannae bear to think of him out there in the dark water all on his own. He should be with his folks. If only he would come ashore…then I can bury him, beside his folks. And then…and then…
(JEAN leaves the raised stage the back way and begins to peg out a selection of black clothes on the line as JANET begins to talk.)
JANET: My three boys, they nearly made it home, but the gale swept their boat past the harbour mouth and onto the rocks in the bay. My boys fought so hard, but the bay was like a pot on the boil and the boat, she flipped over. Robbie and James, they clung to the hull. Robbie lost his grip first. I think – I think the heart had gone out of him when the boat hit. James, my gentle James, he reached down and grasped Robbie's arm and tried to hold him up. After the next wave, they were both gone. Angus now, my fearless boy, he made it to a rock which rises out of the bay like a finger. He hauled himself up and up until he was at the

top. He hung on for an age while we struggled to reach him…but we couldnae…we couldnae… When he knew we couldnae save him and his fingers were too froze to grip the rock, he waited for the next great wave and launched himself ahead of it. My Angus leapt like a salmon, with the wave and the gale behind him. He looked so fierce and strong and he rose so high I thought he would fly right over the bay to us! I put out my arms to catch him… (*She demonstrates.*) …but then the wave curled over and crashed down and took him with it. He never rose again. (*She stops for a moment, overcome.*) When the sea delivered them up, the waves had stripped them of their clothes. All three were slimed with weed and their poor skin was purpled with bruises. Do you know what I thought when I saw them lying there?

I thought of the start of their lives. Aye, that's how they came into the world – naked and purple and slippery wet. Of the twins, James was born first, and he wouldnae stop greeting until Robbie was laid against him. When they came ashore, they were together, for James had never lost his grip on Robbie's wrist. I was glad of that.

My Angus now, when he was born, he leapt shouting into the world – and he left it the same way, leaping and shouting to his death! Ach, when I found him there, on the shore, it pained me to see him lie so still and quiet. Angus was never still in his life! I washed them all myself, and dressed them in their best. I held them in my arms one last time before they went to their coffins. And now, my arms… (*She holds out her arms.*) …they ache so. They willnae stop aching. They ache for something to hold, but my time for holding bairns is past. When my boys died in the bay, I saw all their bairns die with them.

(*JANET remains, arms outstretched, for a few seconds. Then she bows her head. MOLLY stands and moves over to the shelf with the newspaper.*)

MOLLY: My da liked me to read to him from the newspaper when he was home from the fishing. We'd sit by the range, him with his feet in the warming oven until his socks were toasting. (*She tucks the newspaper behind the pipe rack and ca-*

resses the pipes.) He would fill his pipe and light it and listen to me read. (*She stops and sniffs.*) I can smell it now, toasted wool and baccy smoke. I've only to see a newspaper, and that's what I smell. My da, his boat was crippled when the storm hit the fishing grounds. They had no chance of trying to get home. My mam, she looks for Billie now, but she doesnae look for my da. She knows she willnae find him. He wouldnae learn to swim, see, and he carried the stones, to weight his pockets. Aye, some still do that, the older ones, the ones who've seen men drown. He'd say, what's the point in flapping aboot? If you're miles from land in a heavy sea, you're going to go down, however much you struggle. Best get it over quick. I think about my da drowning. I think of how it must have been for him. All fury and hubbub above the water, then…quiet and green and calm. I hope it was calm. I wonder whether he tried to struggle at the end, as his seaboots filled with water and the stones pulled him down? I don't think so. Da was never one to change his mind once he had set his course. He – he liked me to sing to him too. His favourite was a bairn's hymn, about the fishing. It was his favourite because, in the hymn, the fishers never come to harm. They always come home safe. That's how my da wanted the fishing to be for me. Safe. He didnae want me to worry. The fishing is not safe, though. The fishing is an awful dangerous job for a man and it always will be. The sea takes lives. Aye, he loved me to sing that hymn. And, sometimes, when I sang it to him, I think he did feel safe, just for a wee while, sat there with his feet in the warming oven.

Scene 4

A bridging scene between sections three and four.

MOLLY begins to sing the hymn. She sings the first verse alone. The second verse, JANET and JEAN join in humming a harmony. They all sing the third verse and the first three lines of the fourth verse in harmony. A beat, then MOLLY sings the last line alone. Throughout the singing, JEAN turns and begins to search the shoreline, looking for Billy. JANET tries to stop her. JEAN resists, she won't give up. JANET turns away.

MOLLY: When lamps are lighted in the town,
  The boats sail out to sea;
  The fishers watch when night comes down,
  They work for you and me.

  When little children go to rest,
  Before they sleep, they pray
  That God will bless the fishermen
  And bring them back at day.

  The boats come in at early dawn.
  When children awake in bed;
  Upon the beach the boats are drawn,
  And all the nets are spread.

  God hath watched o'er the fishermen
  Far on the deep dark sea,
  And brought them safely home again,
  Where they are glad to be.
  (*As the hymn finishes, JEAN finds a piece of flotsam with part of the name of a boat on it. Holding the piece of wood, she moves along to the end of the gangplank as she recites the names of the boats which were lost. Her voice falters at the name of their boat, then she carries on.*)

JEAN: Forget Me Not. Florida. Beautiful Star. Industry. Radiant. Wave. Guiding Star. Myrtle. Janet. Lass O'Gowrie. Press Home. Six Brothers. Lily of the Valley. Fiery Cross. Sunshine. Margaret and Mary. Blossom. Harmony.
  (*The scene finishes as all three sing the haunting, wordless song with which they opened the play (for example, the Hebridean seal calling song). JEAN goes to sit in the cottage. MOLLY and JANET move off to the back of the raised stage.*)

SECTION FOUR – FEBRUARY

Scene 5

A pause, then JANET moves out onto the floor once more, carrying her bucket. She stops by the front of the raised stage.

JANET: Only a week ago, that spout was hung with icicles. The pump handle was so cold, I had to wrap my hand in my shawl before I could touch it. Today…today, the sun shines. There are snowdrops in the hedgerows. Aye, the seasons turn, just the same. It's been an awful bad winter. So cold. So dark. I thought we'd never come through. Some didnae. Some gave up. The doctor can talk all he wants of pneumonia and weak hearts and such-like. Grief took them. That's the truth of it. (*She moves out to the end of the gangplank.*) We've had arrivals, too, mind, and more to come before the summer. Bairns who will never see their fathers. Old Mary now, she's attended all the births. She's watched every woman take her first look at her bairn. She says they each peer down at this – this wee smudge of a face, all scrunched up and new and no idea yet what its looks will be, and every woman swears the bairn's the image of the man. Well, they must take their comfort where they can. They've precious little else. Most of them havnae even a grave to visit. Thirty bodies – that's all the sea gave back, though we searched and searched. Jean never found young Billie. For months she worked the shoreline at every turn of the tide. Then, one morning the tide turned, but Jean didnae move from her bed. We let her be for a time, then we made her get up, but still she wouldnae eat, or talk, or do a thing. Poor, wee Molly was in such a taking. She thought her mam was going to leave her as well as her da. For a while there, I thought so too – but now…something's changed.

(*As JANET describes JEAN's recovery, we see JEAN getting to her feet. She moves over to the large, family kist at the side of the room. She opens the lid and starts checking through the contents. JEAN carries on sorting throughout the next short scene.*)

Jean's going to the kirk again now and taking an interest in the housework – not like she used to, mind. I hope we never have that again. Aye, she still won't say much, but I think she's coming back.

Scene 6

MOLLY: (*Offstage.*) Janet!

(*JANET turns to watch as MOLLY hurries up to her, clutching a piece of paper in her hand and looking very anxious. MOLLY has changed. The bubbly, child-like quality has gone. She is quieter, more reserved, less self-centred.*) There's a letter come.

JANET: A letter!

MOLLY: Aye. For me. Oh, Janet, what shall I do?

JANET: You can start by reading it to me.

MOLLY: It's from the lassies I was set to crew with this season. They write, 'Molly, we are sorry for your loss and your trouble. You are all in our prayers. We are set to start the season at the end of this month. Do you still wish to crew with us? We have a lass who is of a mind to make a third if you need to stay by your mam.' They ask me to write and tell them…

JANET: Do you still want to go?

MOLLY: Aye. More than anything. (*She pauses, struggling with herself.*) But I think I must stay.

JANET: For your mam?

MOLLY: It near killed her, losing Billie. If I go too –

JANET: Your mam is stronger than you think, lass. She's coming back. Yesterday, she gave me such a telling for using too much of her good oatmeal on the fried herring – it was grand to see her so peeved again. Now who'd have thought I'd ever say that!

MOLLY: Still, I cannae go. Ach, I'll not bother mam with all this. I'll write and tell them no. That's decided.

JANET: Well, listen to you. You grew up while my back was turned.

MOLLY: I'm only wanting to do what's right.

JANET: Aye, I know, and I'm proud of you for it. But you'll not keep your letter from Jean. Not in this place. No, I think we must give your mam a say on this.

MOLLY: Oh, Janet. Do you think we should?

JANET: Like I said, your mam is stronger than you think. Come on, we'll do it now.

(*JANET moves off. MOLLY hesitates, looking anxious,*

then follows JANET. In the cottage, JEAN is still sorting through the large kist. She hears JANET and MOLLY approaching and hastily slams the lid of the kist.)

MOLLY: Janet!

(JANET ignores MOLLY who hurries after her.)

(Hissing.) Janet!

(Both JANET and JEAN ignore MOLLY, who comes to a halt behind JANET.)

JANET: *(Nodding.)* Jean.

JEAN: *(Calm.)* Janet.

JANET: Molly has had a letter.

JEAN: Aye. I know.

MOLLY: Oh, mam, I –

JANET: From the herring lassies.

JEAN: I guessed it.

JANET: They want to know whether she'll be crewing with them this season.

(There is a short silence. JANET and JEAN continue to stare at one another. MOLLY moves closer, gripping her hands together and biting her lip.)

So, Jean. The lass says she will do what ever you want. What do you say?

(JEAN picks up JANET's old travelling kist and brings it to the table where she places it in front of JANET.)

JEAN: She'll not be needing your gift, Janet.

(The hope leaves JANET's face.)

MOLLY: Now, mam, you're not to worry. I'll write to the lassies and tell them I'll not be crewing with them.

JEAN: Aye, you do that Molly. But first I want to explain –

MOLLY: No, mam. You've no need. I know.

JEAN: But I must tell you both –

MOLLY: Hush, mam. No need to upset yourself –

JEAN: Ach, Molly, stop fussing! You're squawking like a silly hen, so you are!

(MOLLY steps back, startled. JANET lifts her head and looks at JEAN again, suddenly full of interest, tension, hope.)

Let me have my say.

MOLLY: But mam –

JANET: (*Stepping forward still looking at JEAN.*) Aye. Let her have her say.

JEAN: You see, lass, when Billie and your da died, I thought I was to blame. I thought – I had not cleaned hard enough.

(*MOLLY stares in horror at JEAN.*)

MOLLY: Not cleaned – ? (*To JANET in a stage whisper.*) See now? See where we have pushed her? Her mind is broken –

JEAN: No, Molly. I am past all that now. See, in all those weeks of searching for Billy, I learned how small I was. I learned I was no more to blame than – than a piece of driftwood on the tide.

MOLLY: Of course you were not to blame –

JEAN: That was an awful bad time. That was the worst time of all. I wanted to die too, then.

MOLLY: Why?

JEAN: Because of the waste! All those years I was so busy working, thinking I was keeping him safe... My lad grew up without me! Remember the Thursday June fairs when you were bairns?

MOLLY: Aye.

JEAN: You and Billie, you'd go off with your da, clutching your pennies, remember? Me I'd stay here, cleaning. You now, you were happy so long as your da was by your side, but Billie, he ached for me to go, so he did. He'd always spend half his money on a sweetie stick for me. Half way through the day he'd rush back home with it. Every year.

'Are you finished yet mam?' he'd say.

'Not yet,' I'd say.

'But you'll come up to the fort in time for the hammer throwing, won't you mam? You'll come to see the races?'

'I'll try,' I'd say. I never made it. After a few years, he knew I'd never come but he still brought me my sweetie stick. He'd tiptoe in and leave it on the table here, then slip out through the door again like a wee summer breeze. I cherished those sweetie sticks, so I did. If you held them up to the window with the sun shining through them, they were the colour of his hair. Shot through with wee bubbles they were and they always had four dents in the stem where he'd clutched them too tight on the way home. There was a pretty wee ribbon tied into a bow around the crook. Pink, green, purple, gold – a different colour every year. I'd make them last for weeks, those sweetie sticks. I'd break off a crumb every now and then and I'd put it on my tongue and I'd sit very still until all the sweetness had melted away. I kept all the ribbons. (*She puts her hand into the pocket of her skirt and brings out a handful of tiny bows, all different colours. She holds them out to the others, cupped in her palm.*) See? Ten of them. Ten years he brought my sweetie stick home for me, until he was fourteen and working on the boat with money of his own and lassies to buy sweetie sticks for instead. (*JEAN lets the ribbons fall to the table.*) Ten years! I wasted ten years when he wanted me by his side. They slipped out of the door behind me like a summer breeze. And now he is gone. How could I have been so foolish?

JANET: Jean – I cannae deny it was an awful waste – but I think you couldnae help yourself. Something had you in its grip –

JEAN: Aye and it took his death to break it.

MOLLY: Oh, mam…

(*MOLLY moves towards JEAN who turns to meet her and grips her by the hands.*)

JEAN: No more waste, Molly. I – I'd like us to be together.

MOLLY: Don't fret, mam, I'll stay –

JEAN: No. No, that isnae what I want. I want…

(*JEAN pulls MOLLY over to the big family kist and lifts the lid.*)

See? It's all packed and ready. I – I want to come too, lass. I want to travel with you.

MOLLY: You?

JEAN: Aye. And you too, Janet, if you'll crew with us.

MOLLY: You, mam? You?

JANET: Me, a herring lassie again…?

JEAN: Are we not a good crew?

MOLLY: Aye.

JANET: We make a grand crew, but Jean – are you sure?

JEAN: No, I am not. I'm feared to leave this place, even
for a wee while. It has always been my home. But, see,
I never got to travel the herring when I was younger. My
da needed me at home after the cholera. I'd like to travel
the herring, even if its only the once. I – I'd like to see all
those grand sights you talk about, Janet. (*JEAN turns to the
table and picks up the little handful of coloured ribbons, holding
them so that the audience can see them.*) Most of all, I'd like
to look up at the sky one night and see those ribbons of
colour dancing across the dark. Do you remember, Janet?
Up at the top of Scotland? I'd
like to hear them shivering and tinkling as if they had hundreds of wee bells caught up in them. All pink and green
and purple and gold… That would be grand… So, shall we
do it? Shall we travel the herring together?
(*MOLLY hugs herself and looks at JANET. JANET walks
over and rubs her hand across the top of her own kist. A
smile spreads over her face.*)

JANET: Aye. We shall.
(*All three women fly together and hug one another laughing
and crying and exclaiming all at the same time.*)

MOLLY: I'll send a letter to the lassies right away.

JANET: Letter? Nay, a telegram! We are busy women now!

MOLLY: Aye! We'll go straight to the Post Office –

JANET: – then we'll call in at the yards to spread the word
among the curers.

MOLLY: Do you think they'll take us on, Janet?

JANET: Aye. (*She lifts her skirts, shows a leg and wiggles her hips.*)
There's many who'll remember me, lass! We'll get work.
(*MOLLY and JANET leave the raised stage, heading
towards the front of the floor space. JANET takes her kist
with her. MOLLY takes the skep that has been serving as
a table. JEAN is left alone.*)

MOLLY: (*Off.*) Mam?

JEAN: Coming!
(*She looks around her home. Throughout her final speeches,
she is moving around, packing stuff away inside the kist*

and the boxes, draping the nets across the boxes, returning the stage to the abandoned state it was in at the start of the play.)

So, that's done then. No turning back now.

(*She smooths her hair and puts on her shawl. She looks at the ribbons for a few seconds, then gently lays them in the kist and closes the lid. Slinging the kist over her shoulder by the strap, she moves to follow the others. The shells catch her eye. Out of habit, she straightens them. She moves off, stops, turns and looks at the shells. She goes back to the mantleshelf. She lifts her arm, hesitates, then picks up one of the shells and puts it on its side on the lower shelf. She stands back, nods.*)

Aye. That'll do.

(*She straightens her shoulders, takes a deep breath, then, head high, she leaves the raised stage. They all turn and look towards the back of the stage as the Northern Lights appear once more, dancing across the sheet which hangs there. The bells tinkle an accompaniment. All three move to stand behind the hanging nets.*)

The End.

SONGS

Song of the Fish Gutters

Come, a' ye fisher lassies, aye, it's come awa' wi' me,
Fae Cairnbulg and Gamrie and fae Inverallochie,
Fae Buckie and fae Aberdeen and a' the country roon,
We're awa' tae gut the herrin', we're awa' tae Yarmouth toon.

Rise up in the morning wi' your bundles in your hand,
Be at the station early or you'll surely hae to stand,
Tak' plenty to eat and a kettle for your tea,
Or you'll mebber die of hunger on the way to Yarmouth quay.

The journey it's a lang ane and it tak's a day or twa,
And when you reach your lodgin's sure it's soond asleep you fa',
But ye rise at five wi' the sleep still in your e'e,
You're awa' tae find the gutting yards along the Yarmouth quay.

It's early in the morning and it's late into the nicht,
Your hands a' cut and chappit and they look an unco' sicht,
And you greet like a wean when you put them in the bree,
And you wish you were a thoosand mile awa' frae Yarmouth quay

There's coopers there and curers there and buyers, canny chiels,
And lassies at the pickling and others at the creels,
And you'll wish the fish had been a' left in the sea
By the time you finish guttin' herrin' on the Yarmouth quay.

We've gutted fish in Lerwick and in Stornoway and Shields,
Warked along the Humber 'mongst the barrels and the creels;
Whitby, Grimsby, we've traivelled up and doon,
But the place to see the herrin' is the quay at Yarmouth toon.

(Ewan MacColl)

When Lamps are Lighted in the Town

When lamps are lighted in the town,
The boats sail out to sea;
The fishers watch when night comes down,
They work for you and me.

When little children go to rest,
Before they sleep, they pray
That God will bless the fishermen
And bring them back at day.

The boats come in at early dawn,
When children wake in bed;
Upon the beach the boats are drawn,
And all the nets are spread.

God hath watched o'er the fishermen
Far on the deep dark sea,
And brought them safely home again,
Where they are glad to be.

(M M Penstone)

Herrin's' Heids

*Add words of each new verse to those of all previous verses

Oh, fit'll I dae wi' the herrin's' heids? I'll mak' them intae loaves o' breid,
I'll mak' them intae loaves o' breid, Sing fal the doo a day.
Herrin's' heids, loaves o' breid, An' a' sorts o' things.

*The herrin' it is the king o' the sea, the herrin' it is the fish for me,
The herrin' it is the king o' the sea, sing fal the doo a day.*

Oh, fit'll I dae wi' the herrin's' eyes? I'll mak' them intae puddin's an' pies,
I'll mak' them intae puddin's an' pies, Sing fal the doo a day.
Herrin's' eyes, puddin's an' pies, Herrin's' heids, loaves of breid,
An a' sorts o' things.

Oh, fit'll I dae wi' the herrin's' fins? I'll mak' them intae needles an' pins,
Herrin's' fins, needles an' pins, *etc.*

Oh, fit'll I dae wi' the herrin's back?
I'll mak' it a laddie an' christen him Jack.
Herrin's' backs, laddies an' Jacks, *etc.*

Oh, fit'll I dae wi' the herrin's belly?
I'll make it a lassie and christen her Nellie.
Herrin's bellies, lassies an' Nellies, *etc.*

Oh, fit'll I dae wi' the herrin's tail? I'll mak' it a ship wi' a beautiful sail.
Herrin's' tails, ships an' sails, Herrin's' bellies, lassies an' Nellies,
Herrin's' backs, laddies an' Jacks, Herrin's' fins, needles an' pins,
Herrin's' eyes, puddin's an' pies, Herrin's' heids, loaves of breid,
An' a' sorts o' things.

SAFE

Characters

LILITH BAKER
a woman in her mid-thirties

JULIE EVANS
twenty five years old, Sean's mother

TIM FORESTER
a man in his late thirties

PETER C. LOCKE
a man in his early thirties, married to Ursula

URSULA LOCKE
a woman in her late twenties, married to Peter

Safe was first performed at Alswick Playhouse on 26 April 2001 by NTC Touring Theatre Company with the following cast:

PETER C. LOCKE, Andrew Crawford

URSULA LOCKE, Jane Dixon

LILITH BAKER, Nicola Berry

TIM FORESTER, Peter G. Reed

JULIE EVANS, Karen Traynor

Director, Gillian Hambleton

Designer, Cath Young

Stage Manager, Craig Davidson

Composer, Jim Kitson

Wardrobe Mistress, Trish Havery

Set Construction, Andy Ross

Scene Painting, Ian Patience

Music

Unless otherwise stated, all music mentioned in the script is from a collection of original music composed for the first production of *Safe* by Jim Kitson. There are pieces suitable for all the fairy-tale, forest, witch, children's and memory scenes. If you wish to use the original music, you can obtain a copy by contacting N.T.C. Touring Theatre Company.

ACT ONE

Opening

*The set should be minimal, flexible and not realistic. It should
suggest the interior of an old dockside warehouse, one which has
serviced the river in a number of different guises over the years, but
which is presently being used as a recycling depot for newspapers,
old clothes, tin cans, glass etcetera. The area will have to double as
a patch of riverside wasteland and also as a forest in some scenes.
There should be a doorway of sorts and a large, brass 'fairytale' key.*

*(N.B. In the first production of SAFE, the company used an
ingenious set, designed by Cath Young, consisting of five doors
on castors. On one side the detail of the door was carved into a
layer of corrugated cardboard. This side was turned to the audience for the warehouse scenes. On the other side, the bottom half
of the door was covered with a mirrored surface with a jagged
top edge to represent recycled glass. The upper half was painted
sky blue. This side of the doors was turned towards the audience
to signal the start of each children's scene. For the forest scenes,
the actors covered the doors with a 'camouflage' net sewn with
scraps of green material to represent leaves. The actors used these
doors for all entrances and exits and also for a series of tightly
choreographed movements – moving the doors back and forth to
change the shape and size of the floor space, or spinning the doors
to signify to the audience whether they were in the warehouse, the
forest or the wasteground. The backdrop for the First Act was a
wall of scrunched-up black plastic rubbish sacks. This set is the
one described throughout the stage directions.)*

*Santana's 'Leave the Lights On' starts to play as the audience
settles and while the house lights are still up. There should be no
stage lighting on so that, when the house lights are dimmed at an
apt point in the song, the audience listens to the lyrics as they sit
in darkness.*

Pause.

71

Out of the darkness comes...a hissing, sibilant whispering, like rustling leaves, like a great forest stirring (this is done by the five actors who are concealed behind the doors). The sounds are disturbing. It could be children – or it could be something else. Music starts to play. In time with the music, a succession of distorted faces appear briefly from behind the doors, lit from below by torches. When the torches are clicked off, the faces disappear.

PETER enters, holding a torch. He is dressed casually in T-shirt and trousers but they are clean and very new-looking. (N.B. All the actors are dressed casually in trousers and T-shirts. The T-shirts carry messages which confirm our first impressions of these characters. For example, in the original production, PETER wore a black t-shirt with 'Kingdom' printed across the chest, URSULA's t-shirt read 'Treat me like a princess', LILITH's, 'Warning: this bitch bites'.)

Scene 1

PETER shines the torch out into the audience, sweeping the beam back and forth, searching for something.

PETER: Excuse me.
> *(The noise stops instantly. A listening pause. PETER continues to sweep the torch beam across the audience.)*
> I think...I might...be lost.
> *(A burst of the sibilant whispering. PETER sweeps his torch beam around the stage, trying to locate the source of the noise. He holds the beam still for a moment, so that it lights up a large brass key on the floor, then he continues his sweep.)*
> I can hear you. I know you're there. Where's the light?
> *(The lights come on, nearly flicker out again, then settle.)*
> That's better. *(He clicks the torch off then turns and looks expectantly around the warehouse. He is alone.)* I know you're there. I heard you. *(He searches the warehouse.)* Kids, is it? You shouldn't be in here. It's dangerous...
> *(He spots a likely hiding place, sneaks up on it and pounces. Nothing.)* Listen. I haven't the time to play silly buggers. You come out now!

(*URSULA emerges from behind a door. She is also dressed in T-shirt and trousers. The T-shirt is oversized, making her look more like a girl than a woman. She is clutching a large book of fairytales to her chest. She hurries to join PETER in the light.*)

URSULA: Don't shout. It's only me.

PETER: Not you. Them. Did you see them?

URSULA: Who?

PETER: Bloody kids. Did they run past you?

URSULA: It's pitch black out there. I couldn't see a thing.

PETER: Bloody kids –

(*He continues his search while URSULA speaks to his back.*)

URSULA: You shot off with the torch while I was still locking the car. I had to feel my way –

PETER: They were here. I heard them. Scrabbling about. Little rats –

URSULA: Rats! Oh, Peter –

PETER: No, not rats –

URSULA: It's just the place for them. And right next to the river –

PETER: Forget the rats. It was kids.

URSULA: But you said rats –

PETER: I meant kids! In a pack, running wild. See? Estate kids, I'll bet. Valleyside's just up the road. They'll be from there.

URSULA: Are you sure?

PETER: I'd put money on it.

URSULA: I mean about the rats –

PETER: There are no rats!

(*There is a sudden, loud burst of the whispering, rather like a flapping of wings. URSULA clutches her book tighter.*)

URSULA: I don't like it here.

PETER: It was only a pigeon.

URSULA: Rats with wings. Let's go home –

PETER: Ursula!

(*He hands her his torch.*)

We're staying. If we help to build this float, the girls are guaranteed a place. They get to ride in the carnival.

URSULA: Yes. About the float –

PETER: Not again.

URSULA: Peter…

(*PETER turns away, checking his watch – an habitual gesture. He unstacks five plastic crates, arranging them in a straight line across the front of the stage area.*)

Peter. Please…

(*PETER looks at his watch again.*)

PETER: It's after seven. We should've started by now.

URSULA: About the carnival–

PETER: Seven o'clock should mean seven o'clock. Not five past. Not ten past. Not, I'll just have one more pint first.

URSULA: Peter!

PETER: That's where he'll be. Still in the pub. Any half-decent organiser would've been here at six thirty, ready to meet and greet. If I ran my business like this, we'd be out on the streets by now.

URSULA: It's a charity, love –

PETER: No excuse for bad organisation.

URSULA: The float, Peter.

(*PETER stops pacing and turns to face URSULA, realising she is not going to let this drop.*)

I still think we should ask the girls first –

PETER: A surprise is better. Imagine their faces.

URSULA: Yes. I am.

PETER: Our girls, up there on the back of the lorry, riding through the crowd, where everyone can see them –

URSULA: That's just the problem.

PETER: Meaning?

URSULA: It's a fairytale float. And they're growing up fast

PETER: Rubbish! They're still our babies. They'll love it.

(*A pause. URSULA stares at PETER who beams back at her, nodding, willing her to agree with him. URSULA hesitates, then gives in, shaking her head and smiling. PETER kisses her on the top of her head.*)

That's my good girl.

Scene 2

Again, PETER looks at his watch.

PETER: You know what? I don't have time for this.
> (*He looks towards the doorway, situated upstage, then down at the large, brass key on the floor. URSULA looks too. They both become very still. Music starts to play, adding to the heightened atmosphere.*)

Pass me that key.
> (*URSULA kneels and picks up the key. She holds the key out to PETER. He takes it and moves towards the doorway.*)

URSULA: What are you doing?

PETER: Beginning.

URSULA: Do you think we should?

PETER: Somebody has to –

URSULA: Are we allowed?

PETER: There's no harm in looking. (*He reaches for the door.*)

URSULA: We don't even know what's in there!

PETER: So let's find out.
> (*PETER swings open the door. The lights go out, leaving them in darkness. The music stops.*)

URSULA: Peter…

PETER: Damn! Give me the torch.

URSULA: Where are you going?

PETER: I think there was a circuit board on the wall back there. You stay put.
> (*PETER moves downstage, shining the torch back and forth.*)

URSULA: Don't be long.
> (*PETER kneels at the edge of the stage area, turning to face upstage. He shines his torch on URSULA's face.*)

Peter?
> (*PETER does not answer. He has effectively 'left' the stage, although he continues to hold the torch beam on URSULA's face.*)

Right. Okay… Okay… (*She begins to hum a tune, then sings to herself, in a hesitant, wobbly voice.*) Moonlight, starlight, the bogeyman's not out tonight –

(*Another torch clicks on behind URSULA and LILITH steps out from behind the door that PETER had tried to open. The witch's music starts to play. URSULA gasps as the beam steadies on her. She cannot see who is beyond the torch beam. LILITH is dressed, like the others, in T-shirt and trousers but, even in casual dress, she looks smart, groomed, a sophisticated woman in contrast to URSULA's girlish looks and dress sense.*)

Who's there?

LILITH: It's all right. I won't bite.

URSULA: Were you – in there?

(*URSULA indicates the open door. LILITH laughs. She begins to walk towards URSULA, causing her to back away.*)

It's just, the lights went. Right after we'd unlocked it. And I didn't hear you.

LILITH: I was going to say something but then you – well – you sang your sweet little rhyme. I thought you might be embarrassed.

URSULA: I mean you didn't make any sound. Not even footsteps. (*She comes to a halt, backed up against the edge of the stage.*)

LILITH: (*Pointing to her feet.*) That's why they're called sneakers. They sneak. Tell you what. Next time I'll whistle.

(*All at once, the lights come on, the music stops, PETER returns triumphant and LILITH switches off her torch, turning to face him with a smile. URSULA is left shaken and wondering why.*)

PETER: Problem solved. Circuit breaker's a bit jumpy, that's all.

(*He sees LILITH and stops. He looks at his watch. LILITH notices.*)

LILITH: Sorry I'm late. I had to dispose of a freshly severed head.

URSULA: Sorry. Did you say – head?

LILITH: One of my better efforts. A lovely frill of torn skin around the neck stump. I even managed a really nice pool of congealed blood on the plate.

URSULA: It was on a plate…?

LILITH: Of course! How else would you serve it?

(*PETER and URSULA share a horrified look. LILITH laughs.*)

Chop, chop… That's what I do…

(*She produces two business cards and presents them to PETER and URSULA*)

'Chop, Chop' Catering. Unusual cakes a speciality. But I also do dinners, parties, weddings –

URSULA: A cake! (*To PETER.*) It was a cake.

PETER: Well, of course it was. Didn't you realise?

(*PETER and LILITH share a superior laugh. PETER hands the torch to URSULA and produces his own business card to give to LILITH.*)

Peter C. Locke, Architect.

LILITH: (*Offering her hand to PETER.*) Lilith Baker.

PETER: (*Shaking LILITH's hand.*) And this is my wife, Ursula.

(*URSULA fumbles the torch and book into one hand and then holds out the other hand, but LILITH has already nodded and dismissed her, turning back to PETER.*)

LILITH: Well, Peter C. Locke, I have high hopes for this float with you running the show.

PETER: I'm not the organiser.

LILITH: No? (*She indicates the open door and the crates.*) I presumed –

URSULA: He – we – shouldn't have, really. It said not to –

LILITH: (*To PETER.*) What's in there?

PETER: I was just about to find out when the lights went out.

LILITH: Shall we?

(*URSULA clutches her book and looks around, as though expecting the organiser to jump out and shout at them. LILITH holds the door open and PETER reaches in and pulls out a box full of oddments.*)

PETER: Is this it? We're supposed to build a float with this?

(*LILITH also looks through the box, finding nothing practical.*)

LILITH: It does seem a trifle optimistic.

PETER: It's a joke. Where the hell is that organiser?

Scene 3

TIM enters, listening to his personal stereo and joining in with the odd phrase. He is wearing a Buffy the Vampire Slayer T-shirt – faded and grubby in contrast to PETER's just-pressed look – and is carrying a joiner's tool bag.

TIM: Beelzebub has a hmm hmm hmm hmm hmmm for me-e-e, for me-e-e, for –
> *(TIM spots URSULA and nods amiably. Over-loud because of the earpieces.)*
Evening!
> *(URSULA indicates that he should take out the earpieces.)*
Sorry.
> *(TIM removes the earpieces, nodding to PETER. Meanwhile LILITH has come up behind him.)*

LILITH: Bohemian Rhapsody?
> *(TIM jumps then turns to face LILITH.)*

TIM: I'm a sad, sad man.

PETER: Where have you been?

TIM: The King's Arms. It's steak pie night.

PETER: *(To URSULA.)* What did I tell you?

TIM: You're not too late. They still had plenty left –

PETER: I am not interested in pie! We've all been waiting for you. I don't have the time –

TIM: Hang on a minute. I've come straight from work. It's not a crime to stop off for a bite to eat.

PETER: The organiser should be here from the start, not stuffing his face down the pub –

TIM: I'm not the organiser.

PETER: I mean, we're all volunteers here. We deserve a bit of –
> *(JULIE enters from behind the last of the five doors. Her T-shirt and trousers are stylish, funky and revealing. She may well have done her own T-shirt design or will have chosen something 'arty' and original.)*

JULIE: Didn't you hear? He said he's not the organiser.

PETER: Are you the organiser?

JULIE: No. I'm bloody not. Who rattled your cage?

URSULA: Peter didn't mean to be rude. Did you, Peter?

PETER: Well! This is sheer incompetence! I just don't –

JULIE: – have the time. You said. (*To TIM.*) Looks like we're in for some fun and games.

TIM: I'm Tim. Tim Forester.

LILITH: Lilith Baker

PETER: Peter C. Locke –

> (*URSULA starts to introduce herself, but PETER beats her to it.*)

– and this is my wife, Ursula.

JULIE: Julie Evans. Is this all of us?

LILITH: I'm afraid it's looking that way.

> (*JULIE pulls a mobile phone from her bag.*)

JULIE: No problem. I can round up a few mates –

PETER: I don't think so.

> (*JULIE shrugs and puts her mobile away again.*)
>
> This is down to the organiser. He should've gathered a good team together –

TIM: She. He's a she. And she gathered me, all right. Gathered me into her arms and gave me a big, soft kiss on the cheek.

LILITH: You know her?

TIM: I was putting up shelves in their offices last week. She knew I'd be useful here. That's why I got the kiss –

URSULA: – and you turned into a prince and rode to her rescue. Just like the fairy tale.

TIM: Sorry?

LILITH: You know. The one where the delusional woman goes around kissing amphibians.

JULIE: It's the other way round for me. They all start off as princes and turn into pond life.

PETER: Where the hell is the woman?

URSULA: We can't start without an organiser. Perhaps we should leave –

JULIE: No way! I chose this as my community project. I've told my tutor and everything. Can't we do something tonight? Anything?

PETER: What with? All we have is a dressing up box and an empty cupboard.

> (*JULIE begins rummaging through the box.*)

LILITH: Maybe we're supposed to fill it.

(*They all turn and look at the shadowy doorway. There is an echo of the sounds heard at the start.*)

PETER: With what?

LILITH: With all the stuff we make for the float.

PETER: And we make it with…?

LILITH: Well (*She sweeps an arm around the warehouse.*) we're not exactly short of raw materials, are we?

JULIE: Oh, yes! Now you're talking.

URSULA: Are we allowed? Is that allowed…?

LILITH: It's a recycling depot. So let's recycle. What do you think, Peter? Surely we can organise ourselves?

PETER: It looks like we might have to.

TIM: What's this float for, anyway?

LILITH: Playsafe are trying to raise funds.

URSULA: For a children's play complex. It's going to be lovely. All fully supervised and protected by a security fence. There'll be a small charge, of course –

JULIE: Just enough to stun them?

URSULA: What? Oh, no, no, not a charge in the fence! I mean an entrance fee. Worth it for peace of mind, don't you think?

JULIE: Where's it going to be, this – complex?

PETER: A stone's throw from here, actually. That scrubby little patch of waste ground down by the river.

JULIE: But – that's where all the kids round here play.

PETER: Exactly. It's time something was done about the place. It's dirty, dangerous, unsupervised –

JULIE: – and they like it just the way it is.

(*A ship's hooter sounds from the river, very loud. The five all look up with shocked expressions.*)

Scene 4

The actors go to stand beside their doors. The ship's hooter sounds again and they turn their heads, listening for an instant. They turn back and spin the doors to the mirrored side. Instantly the scene changes to a patch of waste ground by the river on a summer morning. The lighting becomes bright and sunny and the children's music (reminiscent of fairground music) starts to play. The actors turn their heads to the audience. As though a switch has been flicked, their faces change, lighting up with delighted excitement. They are now five children at the start of a long day of playing together.

(N.B. For the sake of simplicity, the names of the adult characters have been used in the text throughout the children's sequences, but these children are not younger versions of the five adults. They never call one another by name. They are simply a group of nine-year-old children – any child, every child – the child still inside us all. They serve two purposes – they are the 'rude mechanicals' – the light relief – throughout the play – and they serve to remind us of every child's joy in life and willingness to try new things, live in the now.)

The five race to the river bank/edge of the stage and line up, each standing on one of the crates, to wave at the ship as it passes. The music fades.

URSULA: It's massive!

TIM: Cruise liner. Look at all the people!

(*They wave madly.*)

JULIE: Give us a wave!!

PETER: They can't hear you, stupid.

JULIE: Shut up, stupid! Those people did. They're waving. See? And them.

LILITH: And them, and – eeeuuuww!

PETER: What?

LILITH: Look at those two, right at the back –

PETER: It's the stern –

JULIE: They're snogging!

(*They all turn their backs on the ship and make slurping, kissing noises, while doing the 'lovers hands' routine – running their own hands up and down their spines. The hooter sounds again, loud and long. They spin round, line up and wave with renewed enthusiasm.*)

TIM: You know what that sounded like?

LILITH: What?

TIM: A giant fart.

(*They collapse against one another, laughing, then all turn, bend over, point their bums at the ship and, one after the*

other, setting up a rhythm, make farting noises. Once they
are laughed-out, they return to watching, each becoming
quietly entranced by the departing ship, each becoming
totally, unselfconsciously involved in their individual
response, which they all act out simultaneously, the parts
coming together to create a kind of rhythmic music. JULIE
finds an old plank of wood/tree branch/sewage pipe and
begins, practicing basic gymnastic moves and turns, arms
out, toes pointed, singing quietly to herself, repeating the
same phrase over and over.)

JULIE: Ip, dip, dip, my blue ship… Ip, dip, dip, my blue
ship…

(URSULA picks up on the repetition of ship and begins
to improvise a rhyming scheme of her own, jumping from
one place to the next with each new word.)

URSULA: Ship…dip…flip…pip…bip…clip…whip…

(PETER is on the bridge of a ship, staring out to sea. He
lifts binoculars to his eyes and scans the horizon. LILITH
first watches, then imitates, standing close enough for their
shoulders to touch. They pull imaginary levers and consult
imaginary charts, make beeping sonar noises etc.)

PETER: Full speed ahead, Number One.

LILITH: Aye, aye, sir. Full speed ahead…

PETER: Position East by North East

LILITH: Rocks over there, sir.

PETER: Thank you number one. Keep her steady.

LILITH: Steady as she goes, sir.

(Meanwhile, TIM is simply standing still, watching the
ship disappear. URSULA ends her jumping, rhyming game
and comes up beside him.)

URSULA: I wish we were on it. All those little cabins and all
those little beds. And they've got shops and cinemas and
everything. Even a swimming pool.

TIM: But we've been left behind. We're castaways.

URSULA: Yeah! On this island.

TIM: An unin– an unin– A deserted island.

(The others gather round, becoming caught up in the new
game.)

LILITH: And we have to try and survive by ourselves –

TIM: And there's a big forest, with wild animals –

PETER: We should make a base camp –

JULIE: Over here. (*She runs to her chosen place and they all follow her.*) On the edge of the forest. We can use this as a lookout tree. (*She climbs and balances before dropping to the ground again.*)

LILITH: – and this is the bridge to get across the ravine –

TIM: – and it's the only way across because there are sharks.

PETER: – and we can build a real shelter and everything!

URSULA: Little beds and a little table and chairs –

JULIE: And we can live here for ever!

> (*They pause, entranced. The ship's siren sounds again, this time distant and evocative. They turn to look, then they all focus on the audience, giving them a level, considered, knowing stare, as though to say, 'okay we've done that scene, we're going to a different reality now'. This look to the audience will be used to mark the end of every children's scene. The actors return to the doors, spin them in unison to bring the cardboard side round to the audience.*)

Scene 5

The lights change back to the dim lighting of the warehouse. The distant hooter sounds one last time. They turn their heads to listen then go back to the places they were in at the end of Scene Three, picking up the adult story where they left off.

PETER: God knows what they find to do out there. You let kids run wild and they'll get up to mischief –

> (*PETER stops at the sound of breaking glass somewhere in the depths of the warehouse.*)

> See what I mean? Where's that torch?

JULIE: It's only Sean. He's having a bit of a poke about.

LILITH: Sean?

JULIE: My son. I told him to stay close, but you know what they're like. Sean!

PETER: You brought your son?

JULIE: I thought I had… Sean? Come here, now!

> (*PETER looks at URSULA and, obediently, she hurries into trying to explain to JULIE.*)

URSULA: The thing is…in the advert…it said …

PETER: No children.

JULIE: What?

PETER: No children allowed.

TIM: You wouldn't get away with it.

PETER: Get away with what?

TIM: A tutu and pink tights. Not with those legs. Trust me.

PETER: What are you talking about?

TIM: Fairies. We'll need some. On the float. And if children aren't allowed –

URSULA: No, no, no. He didn't mean no children on the float –

PETER: He knows what I meant.

JULIE: My Sean wouldn't be seen dead on a fairytale float. He's come to help build it.

LILITH: Look around you, Julie. Can you see any children?

JULIE: Why? Are you looking for some?

(*A beat.*)

LILITH: Did you read the advert? It said no children at the construction stage. It's a health and safety issue, Julie.

JULIE: I read it! I thought it meant little kids. Sean's nine – and he's good with his hands –

PETER: So we heard.

LILITH: We're all parents here, aren't we?

PETER/URSULA: Yes

TIM: Yes, but –

LILITH: We didn't bring our children, Julie.

(*JULIE turns her back and marches off without a word.*)

Scene 6

TIM: That was a bit harsh

LILITH: Rules are rules, Tim.

TIM: But he's only nine – and she looks about twelve – and we've just told them they can't play with us? I feel mean. We could've found him something harmless to do.

LILITH: Tim, if we allowed that child to stay and he injured himself, we'd be held responsible. Don't get me wrong, I love children –

TIM: But you couldn't eat a whole one?

(*LILITH does not deign to answer. PETER and UR-SULA shuffle, not looking at one another. They are feeling vaguely guilty.*)

The way I see it, we've just lost two helpers – and we're not exactly overrun with them, are we?

(*JULIE returns.*)

JULIE: Right. Sorted.

LILITH: Julie, I thought we'd explained the no children rule –

URSULA: Maybe – since he's already here – a bit of painting…?

JULIE: He's gone.

URSULA: Gone? Where?

JULIE: Well, I had to bribe him with all my money to make him leave, so my guess is he'll be heading for the chippie.

PETER: By himself?

JULIE: Not for long. His mates are like sharks. They can home in on the scent of battered fish from five miles away.

PETER: But, still, he has to get there. By himself. In the dark.

JULIE: There's no pleasing you, is there? I thought you wanted him to go away?

PETER: Not on his own! I assumed you would go with him. What if he gets lost?

JULIE: He won't. He knows his way around here blindfold.

LILITH: Do you live locally, Julie?

JULIE: Valleyside.

(*PETER tut-tuts loudly.*)

(*In an Australian accent:*) Tut, tut, tutut-tut? What's that Skippy? You know, I could swear he's trying to tell me something.

PETER: Valleyside. It figures.

JULIE: Come on, Skippy! Give it to me straight. I can take it.

PETER: All I'm saying is, it's not right, letting kids roam the street at all hours.

JULIE: He won't be. I've told him to be back here by nine.

TIM: Good. That's all right, then.

Scene 7

PETER looks as though he is going to say more. URSULA intervenes, holding up her fairytale book.

URSULA: So, let's choose our story. Any thoughts?

TIM: Snow White.

JULIE: Cinderella.

> (*URSULA nods enthusiastically and begins leafing through her book.*)

PETER: Too scary.

TIM: Scary?

PETER: There are witches in both those stories. We don't want that sort of thing on a kiddies' carnival float.

LILITH: Besides, Snow White and Cinderella, they've both been done to death. We should step off that well-beaten track, don't you think? See what lies in the forest.

> (*JULIE pulls a long, flaxen rope from the box and holds it to her head.*)

JULIE: Rapunzel?

TIM: We can't build a ruddy great tower on a flat bed lorry. Every time we took a corner, there'd be kids flying off it like confetti.

PETER: And there's a witch.

> (*JULIE dumps the rope and lifts out a piece of spiky metal which she places on her head like a crown.*)

JULIE: The Snow Queen, then.

PETER: Another witch.

LILITH: There's always a witch, Peter. You can't avoid them.

URSULA: Oh! I know! What about Hansel and Gretel?

LILITH: You know, that's not a bad idea.

URSULA: It was you who made me think of it.

LILITH: Me?

URSULA: When you talked about seeing what lies in the forest. We could have a clearing with a few trees –

LILITH: (*Mocking.*) And a sweet little gingerbread house.

TIM: A house we could do. No problem.

PETER: There's a witch –

> (*They all turn and look at PETER. He holds up his hands.*)

Hansel and Gretel it is. (*He looks at JULIE.*) Very appropriate, when you think about it.

JULIE: (*To TIM.*) Is he saying what I think he's saying?

TIM: Right. OK. We should start collecting likely stuff –

(*He and URSULA start to work, URSULA casting anxious glances at PETER. The other three ignore them. (N.B. Now they have chosen their story, they will be active in all the subsequent warehouse scenes, collecting materials and creating a cottage of sorts around the doorway, and trees of sorts for the forest. This should not be realistic – just suggestions of windows etcetera.)*)

LILITH: What are you saying, Peter?

(*TIM gives LILITH a look but she is watching PETER with an expression of innocent curiosity.*)

PETER: Hansel and Gretel. You know. Children out on their own. Parents who couldn't care less –

JULIE: I care!

URSULA: Of course you do –

PETER: Care? I've seen whole gangs of them on that estate – some of them little more than toddlers – and not an adult in sight. You call that caring? I mean, why have children if you're not going to look after them – ?

JULIE: OK Mr Peter C. Locke. Mr big, fat-wallet architect. How much are you paying out to keep your kids safe this evening?

(*PETER turns away. He has no answer.*)

LILITH: What does the C stand for, Peter?

(*URSULA's anxiety level rises several notches.*)

JULIE: I can think of a word.

PETER: Nothing. It doesn't stand for anything.

URSULA: (*Holding up something she has found in an attempt to change the subject.*) What about this?

LILITH: It must stand for something. Christopher, maybe?

PETER: It's just an initial.

URSULA: For trees. Is it strong enough…?

JULIE: Cedric? No – Charlie. You look like a right Charlie to me. No? C for –

PETER: (*Shouting.*) Cop-out mother? Couldn't care less? Criminally negligent?

(There is a stunned silence. PETER looks around. They are all staring at him. Realising he has overreacted, PETER clears his throat, looks at his watch. Looks at his watch again.)

PETER: I don't have the time…

TIM: Then let's get started. Will someone check out the back?
(JULIE turns on her heel and exits. TIM nods to LILITH and URSULA. They hesitate, then follow JULIE. TIM turns to face PETER.)

Scene 8

TIM: If you ask me, mate, you're overstepping the mark a bit. You're lucky she didn't clock you one.

PETER: That boy is out there on his own –

TIM: Her boy. Hers. Whatever you think, you can't just – *(He spreads his arms.)* You just can't.
(PETER is silent. He slips his watch off and studies the face. TIM watches him.)

TIM: Nice watch.

PETER: *(Proud.)* Thanks. Top of the range. Kinetically powered. Water resistant to two hundred metres. Accurate to one hundredth of a second. Light as a feather. *(He hands the watch to TIM.)* See? Titanium. Forty percent lighter than steel.

TIM: Nice. *(Comparing it to his own, market stall watch.)* Very nice. *(He hands the watch back to PETER.)*

PETER: Thanks.

TIM: Very nice.
(They are both silent for a moment. PETER studies his watch. TIM stuffs his hands in his pockets. They shuffle.)

PETER: About earlier. Thinking you were the organiser.

TIM: Easy mistake.

PETER: Anyway. I was out of order.

TIM: Yeah, well…

PETER: I just can't stand lateness.

TIM: I noticed.

PETER: I was out of order.

TIM: Yeah, well… (*He slaps PETER on the back.*) Enough said. I'll just… (*He points off stage in the direction JULIE went.*) See how she's doing.
(*PETER nods, then returns to looking at the watch in his hand.*)

Scene 9

PETER continues to stare at the face of his watch Slowly, he sits down, cross-legged. URSULA and LILITH enter to one side. They are in a different part of the warehouse. They begin assessing possible float materials as they talk.

LILITH: So, what does it stand for?
URSULA: Stand for…?
LILITH: The C.
URSULA: I couldn't say
LILITH: Don't you know?
URSULA: Yes. But Peter wouldn't want it spread around –
LILITH: (*Hint of steel.*) Don't you trust me?
URSULA: Yes…
LILITH: Well, then.
URSULA: All right. But you mustn't… You wouldn't… It's – Clearwater.
(*Through the next few exchanges, PETER draws his knees up to his chest and holds the watch up at eye level. He stays in that position, perfectly still.*)
LILITH: Clearwater?
URSULA: His mum chose it. She was –
LILITH: A bit of a hippy?
(*URSULA nods.*)
URSULA: It's from the name of that band. You know –
LILITH: Credence Clearwater Revival? I've heard worse. A friend of mine – he's a bank manager now – his mother called him Heavenly Star Child.
URSULA: You're right. That's worse.
LILITH: They laugh about it now, of course. As I'm sure Peter and his mother do…?
URSULA: She's dead. She died when he was four.

LILITH: Poor Peter. She can't have been that old…?

URSULA: Twenty two. It was drugs.

LILITH: Ah.

URSULA: She used to leave him sitting on a bench at the railway station while she went to get her fix.

LILITH: Shocking.

URSULA: One afternoon, she didn't come back. She was found lying on a rug in the park. People had been walking past her for hours, thinking she was asleep.

LILITH: It's amazing, really, that Peter – Clearwater – Locke has done so well for himself…

(*URSULA looks at LILITH, her face full of a nervous uncertainty. LILITH smiles. They freeze in position as, in his part of the warehouse, PETER begins to sing in a dreamy, stumbling way, as though he is singing a remembered childhood lullabye.*)

PETER: Sit nice and still…

Watch the little hand…

Nice and quiet…

Watch the little hand…

When it reaches four, I'll be back.

When the little hand gets to four.

I promise…

(*PETER stares at the watch face, until TIM and JULIE come back with their finds, breaking the spell. LILITH and URSULA begin to move again and PETER scrambles to his feet, slipping the watch back onto his wrist.*)

Scene 10

PETER: (*To JULIE, urgent, still half in his memories.*) You should go and find him.

TIM: Here we go again.

PETER: Lucy, my eldest, she's the same age as Sean and I don't let her out on her own.

JULIE: A bit slow, is she?

PETER: I beg your pardon?

JULIE: Lyndhurst Dene. Am I right?

PETER: Yes. I have a house in the Dene.

JULIE: Thought so. I work at Anna's Flowers when I'm not at college. It just about pays for Sean's trainers. He wears them out so fast. Must be all that roaming.

PETER: Is there a point to this?

JULIE: I do a lot of deliveries over in Lyndhurst Dene. Floral arrangements for dinner parties mainly… Hey! I could have delivered to your house! Then again, you probably do your own.

PETER: Your point.

JULIE: Those Lyndhurst kids, they come skipping down their driveways every morning, in their Clarks shoes and their Trutex shirts, all shiny and bouncy and full of breakfast, and nine times out of ten, they bounce straight out in front of my van. I've become very good at emergency stops.

(*JULIE advances on PETER.*)

You think you're keeping them so safe. When they finally leave home, they won't know what's hit them. So don't you tell me how to look after my son. At least Sean can take care of himself.

TIM: Well, I'm glad we got that cleared up. Now if you two could give us a hand –

PETER: He's nine years old! You ought to go after him.

JULIE: No.

PETER: You really should –

JULIE: I'm bloody staying!

(*Their gazes lock, then PETER raises his hands.*)

PETER: You're the mother. I've said my piece –

JULIE: Good.

TIM: Thank God for that.

LILITH: Julie. I was thinking. What about Sean's father?

(*TIM and URSULA both look at LILITH. They cannot believe she is stirring it up again. LILITH ignores them.*)

JULIE: What about him?

LILITH: You could give him a call on your mobile. Get him to take Sean home. That way, everybody's happy.

JULIE: I can't do that.

LILITH: Why ever not?

JULIE: I'm on my own.

LILITH: Oh, I see.

PETER: (*Ostensibly to LILITH.*) Single mother. Might have known.

(*JULIE marches over to PETER, close enough to kiss him if she wanted to, leaving only the thinnest space between their bodies.*)

JULIE: You haven't had sex for a very long time, have you?

PETER: Whereas you –

TIM: Okay. I'm gone.

(*TIM picks up his tool bag and heads for the door*)

URSULA: Where are you going?

TIM: Home. There's wrestling on the telly. The fights aren't quite as nasty but the costumes are better.

URSULA: But – we need you.

TIM: What for? To referee?

JULIE: Stay. We're done.

TIM: I'll stay – but only if you promise to play by the rules.

(*TIM looks at each of them in turn. They react with nods or shrugs accordingly. A seagull calls overhead. They look up, then move to the doors. Simultaneously they turn the doors to the mirrored side.*)

Scene 11

The seagull calls again and the lighting changes, becoming a bright day by the river. The children's music begins to play. They look over their shoulders, children once more. Arms outstretched, they swoop around the stage, imitating the flight and the call of the gull. They come to a stop as the music stops and begin the ritual of choosing who is going to be 'on' next. LILITH is in charge of the choosing rhymes, pointing around the circle as she chants.

LILITH: Little Minnie washed her pinnie inside-out. (*She is pointing at TIM when the rhyme ends.*)

PETER: You're on!

(*The others run off, looking for something to climb on for a game of 'tig on high'.*)

TIM: No. I was on last time. And the time before.

JULIE: You were picked. You have to be on. It's the rules.

TIM: I'm not being on!

URSULA: Do it again.

LILITH: Little –

TIM: Do a different one.

LILITH: Ibble –

TIM: Wait… (*He scoots round to a different place in the circle.*)

LILITH: Ibble obble, black bobble,

Ibble obble out

Turn the dirty dishcloth

Inside-out!

(*Once again, LILITH's finger is pointing at TIM. The other four rush away. TIM sulks.*)

PETER: You're on! You're on!

TIM: I'm not playing.

URSULA: Ahhh. Baby isn't playing.

TIM: Shut up!

LILITH: Once more then. Ibble –

TIM: Different. Do a long one.

LILITH: All right, stick in your shoes.

(*They all stick in their right foot.*)

Your shoes –

TIM: Wait.

(*He runs to a different position, pushing one of the others into his original place. LILITH continues and the tension grows with each rhyme ending, each changed foot. TIM is, of course, the first person to have both shoes 'picked'.*)

LILITH: Your shoes are dirty please change them.

(*The others explode out of the circle, heading for the high ground.*)

TIM: I'm not bloody playing!

(*TIM storms downstage and stands in the corner, his back to the others. They look at one another. LILITH comes over and stands behind him. She rests her chin on his shoulder.*)

Bog off!

(*LILITH backs off slightly, then has an idea.*)

LILITH: Can you do this?

(*TIM turns round and laughs at the grotesque face she is pulling. They all try to copy her, including TIM. The upset is forgotten as they each wheel out their 'party pieces'*)

*(anything from the athletic to the grotesque) one at a time,
challenging, 'Can you do this?' They end up on their backs
on the floor and stay there, content to be quiet for a while
and watch the clouds.)*

URSULA: *(Pointing.)* That cloud looks like a castle

JULIE: There's a dragon

PETER: And a smiley face, look.

TIM: And that one looks like a big, fat arse.

(General collapse.)

TIM: Look, it's even got a bum hole in the right place. See
that bit where the sky shows through?

PETER: Blue poo!

*(More collapsing and repeating of 'blue poo'. Finally, they
quieten and climb to their feet…)*

LILITH: What shall we do now?

*(The seagull calls again and they all look up, then again
that level stare out into the audience. They move back to
the doors, turn them back to the warehouse side.)*

Scene 12

*The seagull calls, they look up, then turn back to their adult roles
in the warehouse.*

URSULA: There are plenty of parts. Hansel and Gretel, of
course. Then there are all the little forest creatures.

JULIE: I could make some cool costumes. Squirrels, badgers,
that sort of thing.

LILITH: Could I suggest – ? My son, James, would make an
excellent Hansel. *(She produces a photograph.)* Here he is.
He's six years old.

*(LILITH hands the photo to URSULA. PETER leans
over to look.)*

URSULA: Oh, he'd be perfect. He's lovely!

*(PETER pulls a photograph from his wallet and hands it
to LILITH. JULIE looks over LILITH's shoulder.)*

PETER: That's Lucy. She'd make a good Gretel.

JULIE: Bit old for that sort of thing, isn't she?

URSULA: That's what I thought –

(*PETER gives URSULA a look, then pulls another photo from his wallet.*)

PETER: Sophie for Gretel then. She's only six.

LILITH: Ah, sweet! What a little sugar plum. Couldn't you just eat her up? Do you have a photo of Sean, Julie?

JULIE: No. And before you nab Gretel for your little girl, what about Tim?

TIM: I don't look good in plaits.

JULIE: Not you, you wally! Your daughter.
   (*TIM laughs.*)
   What?

TIM: Alice is as tall as I am and she scowls. A lot.

URSULA: How old is she?

TIM: Twelve.

URSULA: Twelve! We've got that to come. All those hormones kicking in.

TIM: Hormones. You know there's one which makes it almost impossible for her to move her lips? And then there's another which gives her this really strong urge to go out in the middle of winter dressed in nothing but a handkerchief and a pair of pants.
   (*The others are laughing when he adds:*)
   Besides, she won't be around this Easter. Her mother's taking her away. For the holidays.
   (*The laughter tails into silence.*)
   We're divorced. Three years now. But that's okay. Really. I get to see Alice every week. (*He points to his Buffy T-shirt*). We're both Buffy fans. I've got all the boxed sets. We watch them together.

LILITH: That's lovely. It's lovely to have a shared interest.

TIM: Yeah. Lovely.
   (*TIM smiles down at the floor. The others exchange glances.*)

PETER: Right. Trees… Trees…
   (*PETER, JULIE and URSULA get busy. LILITH remains still, holding the photograph of James. TIM, looking for a distraction, leans over to look at the photograph.*)

TIM: Your son?

LILITH: James.

(*TIM frowns, looks more closely, glances at LILITH then stares intently at the photo with a confused expression.*)

TIM: He's called James…?

(*LILITH snatches the photo away and stuffs it into her pocket. She hurries away, throwing nervous glances at TIM.*)

Scene 13

URSULA holds out her fairytale book

URSULA: Shall I –

LILITH: (*Jumping in.*) What a good idea! We can listen while we work. (*Glancing at TIM who is still watching her.*) Whenever you're ready…

URSULA: Once…

(*The fairytale music starts to play. URSULA stops briefly and raises her head. The others all follow suit. They have caught a suggestion of the change which is about to sweep through the warehouse. An expectant pause, then…*)

…upon a time…

(*As URSULA continues reading, the change begins. Magic is flowing through the warehouse – not a tinselly, sparkly friendly sort of magic, but a dark and powerful force of transformation. URSULA reads on as TIM, LILITH, PETER and JULIE drape the doors with camouflage nets of leaves and move them into position for the forest scene. The whole scene becomes heightened as they disappear behind the 'trees'.*)

…a poor woodcutter and his wife lived on the edge of a –

ALL: – great, dark forest.

URSULA: And they had two children.

(*JULIE emerges from behind her tree, turning as she goes. When she faces the audience again, she has made her arms into a cradle.*)

URSULA/JULIE: A boy…

(*TIM duplicates JULIE's movement, ending up standing beside her, both downstage.*)

URSULA/TIM: And a girl...

URSULA: And they felt their hearts both soar and shiver as they cupped the frail necks of their babes and kissed their delicate skulls and relished –

(*TIM and JULIE both raise their cradled arms to their faces, close their eyes and take a long, hungry breath in.*)

– their sweetness. And, like all parents, they promised. How they promised.

JULIE: Close your eyes. I'll keep you safe.

TIM: Go to sleep. I'll keep you safe.

JULIE/TIM: For ever and ever...

URSULA: They had little enough to break or bite but they gave all they could to their children. And the children ate and grew and ate and grew and the parents worked hard at keeping their promises.

(*The next few exchanges should be fast and frantic as JULIE, TIM, PETER and LILITH take turns at swinging their doors open, shouting an instruction and pulling the doors shut again.*)

JULIE: Hot! Hot!

TIM: Watch that step –

LILITH: Away from the edge –

PETER: Not with that in your mouth!

JULIE: Be good.

TIM: Listen to the teacher.

LILITH: Helmet on!

PETER: Watch the road –

JULIE: Does it have seat belts?

TIM: You can't go out like that!

LILITH: What's his name?

PETER: Where does he live?

ALL: (*Except URSULA.*) What time will you be back?

URSULA: And all the while, the great, dark forest and all the creatures in it sprawled around the little house. Waiting. The forest knew all about parents and their promises.

Scene 14

LILITH and PETER remove the camouflage nets from the doors and return them to the warehouse positions. URSULA puts down the book and joins them. LILITH, PETER and URSULA then exit. TIM sorts through a box. JULIE paces. TIM has found a tabloid newspaper and proceeds to flick through it as JULIE talks.

JULIE: I mean, what is his problem?

TIM: He's a prat. Ignore him.

JULIE: Sean can look after himself out there. He'll be back. He always comes back.

TIM: Of course he does.

JULIE: He has no right.

TIM: Of course he doesn't.

JULIE: I'm not a bad mother!

TIM: Of course you're not.

JULIE: I mean, I lose my temper sometimes. Doesn't everybody?

TIM: Of course they do.

(JULIE stops, finally catching on to TIM's automatic replies. She gives him a look. He straightens, folds and drops the paper, then perches on the side of the box, giving her his full attention.)

JULIE: When he was a baby, there were times… You know that screaming they do? That screaming? Hours and hours with the dark outside the window and the whole world asleep except me… And him… I used to pretend he wasn't my baby. Can you believe that? There'd been a mix up at the hospital. Sean was lying in another cot, all peaceful and quiet, and I was left with this screaming – thing. On the worst nights, he stopped sounding human. He was just this howling, sucking monster and I wanted to –

TIM: – but you didn't.

JULIE: I packed a bag for him once. Wrote a note. 'Please look after this child…' I even put serious thought into which shop doorway it should be. The delicatessen? Marks and Spencer? You see, I am a good mother. I always wanted the best for him.

TIM: You shouldn't do this now. You had to stay for your

project. Your tutor's expecting a report –

JULIE: Sod my tutor! I sent Sean out into the dark for the sake of a 'Good start, Julie' from a man who still wears corduroy trousers!

TIM: We've all got one you know.

JULIE: What?

TIM: A guilt supply. You. Me. Even Peter C. Locke. It's non-returnable. And you never run out of it. I don't know where Alice is right now. There are days and days when I don't know where she is. I can make a few good guesses. She's probably watching telly with her mum. Or up in her room doing her homework. But she could be out with her friends. And they might have nicked a bottle of vodka. And they may be thinking a game of chicken on the railway line would be a really good laugh… I used to be on the phone to my wife – my ex-wife – all the time. I don't do that now. I have to trust that Alice is safe. I have to trust she can look after herself.

(*JULIE nods.*)

JULIE: Like Buffy.

(*TIM looks down at his T-shirt.*)

Teenage girls kicking ass. Comedy monsters. Reassuring. That's why you like it. Isn't it?

Scene 15

LILITH, PETER and URSULA enter. LILITH is carrying an armful of brightly coloured paper and strips of cut-out dolls. TIM moves in front of JULIE to give her a chance to compose herself, but LILITH does not miss a thing.

LILITH: What's the matter, Julie? Is it Sean? It must be worrying, not knowing where he is.

TIM: What about your son, Lilith? Where's he right now?

LILITH: (*Uncomfortable.*) James? He's at home.

(*She turns away and begins to decorate the witch's 'house'. The others join her, using the coloured paper and the strips of cut-out dolls. They do not notice the tension developing between TIM and LILITH.*)

TIM: With your husband?

LILITH: He's with his father, yes.

TIM: Usual routine is it? Bath, bed and story?

LILITH: Pass me a handful of those paper strips, would you, Ursula?

PETER: I don't suppose you get to be in on that too often, what with all your functions and dinner parties.

TIM: Who looks after James then? His father?

LILITH: Yes.

URSULA: Ahh. That's sweet.

TIM: Sweet.

(*LILITH squares up to TIM.*)

LILITH: You know what, Tim…?

(*A pause while they match stares, then LILITH backs down.*)

There's a roll of cellophane in the back. If we cut it into squares, it would look like sugar pane windows.

(*LILITH begins to exit, then pauses. She looks at PETER, then JULIE.*)

Julie? Give me a hand would you?

(*JULIE is reluctant, but follows LILITH out. TIM watches them go. URSULA and PETER have noticed nothing. TIM returns to working on the witch's 'house' with them. URSULA picks up a strip of the cut-out dolls. She pauses, studying them.*)

URSULA: They must be really close, James and his dad.

PETER: It's not the same as fathers and daughters though, eh, Tim? Now me and my girls – that's a really special bond.

URSULA: Like me and my dad. We did everything together. I think mam felt a bit left out sometimes. I do miss him.

PETER: Now, Ursula. Don't start.

URSULA: I won't. I'm only remembering. No harm in that, is there Tim?

TIM: No harm at all.

URSULA: Big and cuddly, he was, like a teddy bear. He liked his cooked breakfasts. What about you, Tim?

TIM: I'm a toast and coffee man.

PETER: Pity he wasn't. He might still be here.

URSULA: Peter!

PETER: Heart attack. Wallop!

URSULA: I was right in the middle of my exams. I was going
to go on to teacher training and everything. I couldn't be
bothered after that. We used to dance together, me standing on his feet. Huge feet, he had. And hands like big
paws.

(*URSULA begins to turn, holding the cut-out dolls out
in front of her.*)

He'd grab hold of my hands and we'd waltz around, faster
and faster, until I was dizzy and begging him to stop. 'Hold
on,' he'd shout. 'You'll be fine! Just hold on!'

(*PETER moves over and gently removes the dolls from
URSULA's hands. TIM looks away. LILITH and JULIE
return, carrying a square of cellophane each. JULIE is
looking much happier.*)

JULIE: There you go, Peter. (*She holds up the square.*) Is that –
clear enough for you?

(*URSULA looks at LILITH, instantly suspicious, but
LILITH will not meet her eye.*)

PETER: (*Taking the cellophane.*) Thanks.

JULIE: This complex they're going to build. On our waste
ground –

PETER: No. You see, legally it's not yours. It belongs to the
council –

JULIE: Whatever. I was thinking, they're not going to need all
of it, are they?

PETER: Oh, I think they will. It's not that big a piece of land.
And they'll need a fair-sized car park.

JULIE: A car park? For a kid's play area?

PETER: They'll have to be driven there, won't they? You
can't expect children to travel far on their own these days.
It's not safe.

(*As the first notes of 'Thus Spake Zarathustra' sound, the
actors pause, listening, then they head for the doors and
turn them to the mirrored side.*)

Scene 16

The lighting changes. They are children again, on the wasteground. Throughout the first part of this scene Thus Spake Zarathustra continues to blast out as the five simulate a rocket launch using the mirrored doors and their own bodies. As the music builds to the finale, they imitate the effect of increasing G-forces.

PETER: Starting launch countdown.
JULIE: Beginning ignition sequence...
PETER: Ten... Nine... Eight...
TIM: Booster rockets activated.
PETER: Seven... Six...
LILITH: Navicom online and responding...
URSULA: Houston we are go for launch!
PETER: Five...
JULIE: Four...
LILITH: Three...
TIM: Two...
PETER: One...
EVERYONE: Lift off!

> *(The music ends and the five move slowly apart, moon walking. They spread out across the front of the stage area, studying the audience with a mixture of puzzlement and disgust and sharing horrified glances. Finally, TIM imitates the crackle and static hiss of a radio transmission, talking into his cupped hand to get the correct tinny sound. The others follow suit, imitating the static and crackle etcetera throughout the next few exchanges.)*

TIM: It's life, Captain, but not as we know it.
URSULA: Should we take samples?
LILITH: *(Eyeing the audience.)* Could be dangerous.
PETER: Set phasers to stun and get ready to move in.

> *(They set imaginary phasers and prepare to move in on the audience. At this point JULIE makes her first attempt at 'transmitting' but her imitation of the static crackle goes badly wrong, coming out more like a strangled quack. The other four stop in their tracks and turn to stare at her. Embarrassed, JULIE tries again. Once again she can only produce a strangled quack. The others get the giggles.)*

JULIE: What…? What!
TIM: Houston, we have a problem.

(*JULIE abandons the moon walking, folds her arms and turns her back, in a huff.*)

URSULA: One of our team appears to be mutating…
PETER: Turning into…
LILITH: Donald Duck!

(*They gather around JULIE, quacking. JULIE attempts to remain in a huff but finally joins in. They stop suddenly, turn to the audience, level a stare at them, then go to the doors and turn them to the warehouse side.*)

Scene 17

Back in the warehouse, JULIE and PETER continue their conversation about children and transport as though there has been no interruption.

JULIE: There's buses.
PETER: Public transport? No thank you.
JULIE: You won't give an inch, will you?
PETER: I care about the safety of my children –
JULIE: And I don't?
PETER: All I'm saying is, it's not enough just telling them about the dangers out there. They're not listening. Not really. Because they don't think death applies to them. The trouble with kids is they think they can live forever.
JULIE: The trouble with us is we think we know better.
PETER: What the hell is that supposed to mean?

(*PETER and JULIE are once again squaring up to one another.*)

URSULA: Coffee break, don't you think?
TIM: Good idea. I'm parched.

(*PETER turns his back and picks up the first thing that comes to hand the tabloid newspaper that TIM was flicking through earlier. PETER pretends to be reading it.*)

JULIE: What's the matter, Peter? Don't you like coffee? I'm sure we could find something else. What about a reviving glass of – clearwater…?

(*PETER spins around, a look of shock on his face. JULIE*)

laughs as she exits. URSULA stares at LILITH who shrugs, then leaves too. TIM follows her, a look of puzzlement on his face. PETER turns to URSULA and slowly shakes his head. She hesitates, then scuttles off, head down. The 'memory/heartbeat' music begins to play as PETER slowly rips the newspaper apart. At some point he notices a headline and the ripping becomes controlled, purposeful. Carefully, he tears out the headline and places it to one side, discarding the rest of the page. He finds another headline, and another, giving them the same treatment. The lights dim and he leaves the stage. The 'memory/heartbeat' music stops. 'Bad Moon Rising' by Creedence Clearwater Revival plays us into the interval as the house lights come up.)

End of Act One.

ACT TWO

Scene 1

*Two of the doors are centre stage, side by side, with the 'forest'
camouflage nets draped over them (N.B. crates should be set behind
these two doors so that the actors can appear above the tops of the
doors). The other three doors are set upstage, acting as the door
and windows of the witch's house. The lighting is low – the same
lighting as is used in all the fairytale scenes. The atmosphere is
heightened. The five walk back on in silence, three from one side,
two from the other. TIM and JULIE are each carrying a pair of
shears or scissors of some sort, which they hold down at their sides.
The blades snicker-snak loudly as they open and close. TIM and
JULIE stand one on each side of the doors, facing the audience.
PETER and URSULA disappear behind the remaining three
doors, which are positioned upstage. LILITH stops at one side,
downstage, and picks up the fairytale book. The witch's music
begins to play as she opens the book.*

LILITH: And Hansel and Gretel stumbled through the forest,
calling, calling to the parents who had lost them.
*(TIM and JULIE step behind the two downstage doors as
PETER and URSULA emerge from the upstage doors,
one each side. They move downstage, backing towards one
another, scanning the forest.)*
PETER: Mam?
URSULA: Daddy?
*(They bump into one another and – without looking round –
grasp hands for mutual support, still calling, still searching – in
a neat encapsulation of PETER and URSULA's married life.)*
PETER: Mam!
URSULA: Daddy!
LILITH: And the children lay down in the thickest part of the
forest. Lay down by the fire and slept.
*(PETER and URSULA kneel down together in front of
the two 'forest' doors, facing the audience.)*
– and when they woke, the fire had –

105

LILITH/PETER/URSULA: – died –

URSULA: – down to –

LILITH/PETER/URSULA: – cold ashes –

LILITH: – and the dark came –

(*TIM and JULIE emerge above the tops of the 'trees',
menacing, monster-like, curling their fingers into the
camouflage netting.*)

LILITH/TIM/JULIE: – creeping –

URSULA: – through the forest –

(*'HANSEL' and 'GRETEL' are very afraid, but they do
not look round.*)

LILITH: And Hansel comforted his sister, saying, 'Only wait
until the moon comes out. Then we shall see the crumbs of
bread which I have dropped and they will show us the way
home.' But when the moon shone, they could not see any
crumbs. Something had –

LILITH/TIM/JULIE: – eaten them!

LILITH: And now Hansel and Gretel were very afraid, for
they knew that crumbs can only whet – (*Knives being sharpened. Scissors snapping shut.*) – the appetite. And for all the
hungry monsters in the forest that night, children –

(*LILITH/TIM/JULIE all take a long, deep breath in,
testing the air.*)

– soft and tender children – were the tastiest meat of all.

(*LILITH leaves the book and moves to stand at the side of
one of the 'forest' doors, joining TIM and JULIE. 'HAN-
SEL' and 'GRETEL' cling together, each facing outwards.
LILITH/TIM/JULIE share out the following lines – repeating, echoing, creating a feeling of building menace.*)

Would you like to see it? Would you? I'll show you if you
want. Would you like to touch it? Touch it. Touch it. Don't
cry. Eat it all up! Oh yes. Would you like to touch it? Touch
it. Touch it. Would you? Would you like a sweetie to suck?
Come here.

(*LILITH, TIM and JULIE again take a long, deep breath,
to pick up the scent.*)

LILITH/TIM/JULIE: Come here!

(*'HANSEL' jumps up and runs off. 'GRETEL' spins to*

face the forest doors.)

URSULA: (*Looking in the direction PETER took.*) Daddy!

LILITH/TIM/JULIE: (*To URSULA.*) Are you sure you want your daddy, little girl?

URSULA: Yes –

LILITH/TIM/JULIE: Certain sure?

(*URSULA is looking around with a growing dread.*)

URSULA: Yes. No… (*Turning back to face the audience, still on her knees.*) I don't know.

LILITH: Here he comes, little girl. The worst monster in the forest.

TIM: Your daddy – the bear.

JULIE: The beast that walks like a man.

(*URSULA scrambles to her feet as TIM, LILITH and JULIE move off, moving the doors and crates off with them, one door to each side of the stage. They exit behind these two doors as the lights return to normal.*)

Scene 2

URSULA is no longer 'GRETEL'. She is back in the warehouse, but she is disorientated and disturbed. She keeps looking behind her at the witch's cottage they have created. PETER enters, ready to confront URSULA about giving away his middle name. He is very much in the present, whereas URSULA is in a world of her own, struggling with an emerging childhood memory. She looks once again at the witch's house.

URSULA: Safe as houses?

PETER: Did she have a good laugh, then, when you told her?

URSULA: Safe as my house…?

PETER: So much for loyalty

(*PETER exits.*)

URSULA: Turning back to face the audience…my house… It's my house…

(*A lower, minor key version of the children's 'fairground' music (or, alternatively, the 'memory/heartbeat' music) plays as URSULA begins her next speech. The door acting as the cottage door opens and URSULA's 'memory' father steps out (a life sized 'puppet' worn/manipulated by the actor playing TIM). The face and body of the puppet are superimposed onto the material in the simple, distorted style of a child's painting – the sort of painting where the mum and dad and children and pets are all lined up outside their house beneath a thin blue line of sky and a sunflower sun. The figure is smiling but this painting has gone slightly awry and the result is disturbing.)*

He grabbed my hands. Held them in his big paws. Held them tight. I was begging him to stop – but he wouldn't. Faster and faster he went. 'Hold on. You'll be fine. Just hold on. That's it…'

(The father figure wraps his arms around himself and runs his hands up and down his body in a grotesque echo of the 'lover's hands' routine the children enacted earlier.)

Afterwards, he took me to the fair. Because I was his good girl and he was my daddy again. I rode the merry-go-round –

(The father figure raises an arm and waves in a slow, stylised manner, waving to his daughter on the merry-go-round. URSULA waves back.)

I rode the merry-go-round and my daddy waved and I waved back. 'Hold on! Hold on tight!' Round and round until I was dizzy. And my daddy waved. My daddy…

(The father figure waves one last time and backs off until he can pull the door shut, obscuring him from view. URSULA stares out into the audience for a long moment as the music fades.)

Scene 3

PETER enters upstage and stands studying the binliner backdrop.

URSULA: Peter…?

(PETER yanks down the backdrop a section at a time, revealing a second black backdrop with white strips marking out the outline of a cottage. The strips – and the white windows and door – are lettered in black with tabloid newspaper headlines. They are all to do with missing,

raped or murdered children. URSULA stares at the thing PETER has created, then she turns to study PETER. A change is coming over her. She is reassessing the value of being a 'good girl'.)

PETER: (*Pointing at the headlines on the front of the house.*) This is what happens. See? This is what she's risking every time she lets that boy out on his own.

URSULA: It'll worry Julie when she sees those. Is that what you want?

PETER: Yes! She needs to be worried! (*Holding out his wrist for URSULA to see his watch.*) Have you seen how long that child has been missing?

URSULA: Not missing. Not yet. They're only missing when they're overdue.

PETER: Alone, then.

(*URSULA goes closer to study the headlines. They make grim – and sensational – reading.*)

URSULA: (*With a premonitory shudder.*) What are you making, Peter?

PETER: (*Sullen.*) I'm doing it for the boy.

URSULA: Or to wipe the grin from her face. (*She steps closer.*) Peter. Sometimes the monsters aren't out there. (*She lays a hand on his chest.*) Sometimes, they eat you from the inside…

(*They share a look, honest, naked, rare, as equals – it contrasts with the lack of intensity between them since they arrived at the warehouse. PETER turns away.*)

Who's it really for, your – lesson? Julie – or your mother?

(*PETER picks up the pile of tabloid headlines he ripped from the newspaper at the end of Act One. He walks a winding path around the stage area, screwing up each headline after he has read it out and dropping the balled paper to the floor. They glow under the lights, like Hansel's trail of pebbles.*)

PETER: 'Home-alone boy asked neighbours for food.'

URSULA: Why have you kept it, Peter?

PETER: 'Boy found tied to cot while mother shops.'

URSULA: That letter C?

PETER: 'It was heroin, admits mother of fire death boy.'

URSULA: Curled up nice and safe, right in the centre of your name.

PETER: 'Clubbing means more to me than my own son.'

URSULA: Curled up right in the heart of it.

> (*PETER comes to a stop at the front of the stage. He speaks slowly, attempting to keep control of himself.*)

PETER: I kept it because it makes my name sound more dignified.

> (*URSULA reaches up, cups his face in her hands and looks into his eyes. They stay like that for a long moment, then PETER snatches his head away.*)

That's all. Because it's more dignified.

Scene 4

URSULA bows her head and leaves the stage. The 'memory/heart-beat' music starts to play as the cottage door opens and PETER's 'memory' mother steps out – again a life-sized, child's-painting 'puppet' (again worn/manipulated by the actor playing TIM). The mother follows the 'pebbles' of screwed up newspaper towards PETER as JULIE, URSULA and LILITH each say their lines from behind their doors. PETER will not look round. Instead he removes his watch and holds it in his hand, staring at the face, desperately trying to hang on to that ever-weakening self-control.

JULIE: And because she sang to you…

URSULA: And because she loved to brush your hair…

LILITH: And because she listened to your stories…

> (*As JULIE says the next line, PETER suddenly claps his hands to his ears and uses his voice to drown out the last two words, the way children do when they don't want to hear something.*)

JULIE: And because you –

PETER: Nananananana!

JULIE: – loved her. You still –

PETER: Nananananana!

JULIE: – love her.

> (*The mother holds out her hand to PETER, but he clutches the watch hard and refuses to turn round. She goes back behind the door. PETER gets himself under control, then he straps the watch back on, checks it, smooths his hair, lets out his breath.*)

Scene 5

JULIE storms on stage with TIM and LILITH, followed by URSULA.

URSULA: Julie, wait! He's only trying to make you see –
    (*JULIE marches up to the headlines, reads. Then she turns to face PETER.*)
JULIE: You're sick.
URSULA: He's only –
JULIE: You're bloody sick!
PETER: No. The sick ones are out there. With your son.
JULIE: You bastard!
PETER: Does he know about the railway bridge? Have you warned him to keep away?
JULIE: (*Softer, uncertain, closer to tears.*) You bastard…
PETER: Does he know about the wino's there? About the one they can never catch? The one who likes little boys?
    (*JULIE is crumbling. The other three watch, appalled.*)
    What about the park? Does he know not to go in the park at night? Does he know about the incident in the trees behind the swings? Does he?
TIM: That's enough. That's more than enough.
    (*JULIE is distraught. Everyone is uneasy now, looking at their watches, looking out at the dark. A moment, then LILITH puts a voice to their uncertainty.*)
LILITH: We could go looking for him.
URSULA: Yes. Just a quick scout around…
JULIE: (*Quietly.*) No.
TIM: It's no bother –
JULIE: No! He's not late. He doesn't deserve to have five people walking the streets, calling out his name. He deserves to be trusted.
    (*JULIE looks at TIM for reassurance, remembering their earlier conversation. TIM nods.*)
    I – trust him.
PETER: But, I'm trying to tell you. (*He points to the clippings.*) It's not about trust. I'm trying to tell you what's out there –
JULIE: It is! It is about trust! I know there are monsters. And sometimes, hardly ever, somebody's kid is going to run

111

into one. I know that! But we have to trust it won't happen. It's what we have to do. It's all we can do. And you're
wrong. Kids don't believe they're going to live for ever.
They just act like it. It's what they have to do. And you
know what? They're brilliant at it compared with us.
(*JULIE turns her back on PETER and exits behind one
of the doors.*)

PETER: I don't understand her. Why won't she listen? He
could be out there now, on her precious waste ground with
all the dirt and the rusty metal. He could have fallen in the
dark. He could be hurt, with no-one there to clean him up.
He could be hurt!

Scene 6

JULIE calls from behind her door.

JULIE: Coming, ready or not!
(*The children's music starts as they all run to the doors
and spin them to the mirrored side, hiding behind them in
the process. Only URSULA does not hide behind her door.
Instead she covers her eyes with her eyes.*)

URSULA: One mississippi, two mississippi, three mississippi... Coming, ready or not!
(*The music stops. There follows a game of hide and seek,
where URSULA stalks the others and, one by one, they
break cover and reach 'home'. PETER is the last to make
a run for it. Just as URSULA is about to catch him, he
falls, badly. He lies still, curled up and silent. The others
have frozen, as children do when they are scared. For a long
moment, they watch PETER's still body. Then he begins to
wail. He sits up, clutching his elbow and the wails increase
in length and volume. URSULA becomes motherly and
efficient. The others gather round to watch.*)
Let me see.
(*PETER wails and shakes his head, clutching his elbow
tighter.*)
Come on.
(*URSULA reaches for PETER's arm but he wails even
louder and shields it from her. URSULA retreats.*)

I won't touch it. I just want to look.

(*PETER shakes his head, still wailing. URSULA suddenly belts him across the back of the head. PETER is shocked into silence.*)

Show me!

(*PETER sticks out his arm and they all crowd round.*)

It's only a scrape. I'll soon fix that. We need…a dock leaf.

(*LILITH, TIM and JULIE scatter, searching the waste ground. LILITH finds a leaf.*)

LILITH: I've got one!

URSULA: Right, now. We put some soil in it… (*She scoops dirt into the leaf.*) …and then we all have to spit in it.

(*URSULA holds out the leaf to each of them in turn and they all solemnly spit into it.*)

Now I mix it all together… There!

(*Proudly, URSULA holds the leaf out to PETER, who takes it but hesitates.*)

Go on! It'll stop it hurting.

(*PETER slaps the leaf onto his elbow, then smiles and wipes his nose on his sleeve.*)

See? Now you have to lie down for a while.

(*PETER lies down and URSULA finds something on the waste ground to cover him with. Then she gets under the covering with him. A fair amount of wriggling and giggling begins. LILITH, TIM and JULIE turn their backs on PETER and URSULA and sit down in a row in front of them, facing the audience. TIM is in the middle of JULIE and LILITH, who are both simpering at him for all they are worth. He looks from one to the other, finally choosing to edge, ever so casually, towards JULIE. LILITH turns her back on them and folds her arms, in a sulk, but she can't resist turning back to watch. With excruciating slowness, TIM edges closer until he can reach out and tuck JULIE's hair behind her ear. JULIE closes her eyes and waits for the expected kiss on the cheek. Very seriously, TIM pokes his tongue right out of his mouth, then, holding his tongue rigid, he leans over and sticks it in JULIE's ear. JULIE's eyes shoot open. She spins round and punches him in the chest, very hard.*)

TIM: Ow!

(*LILITH laughs. JULIE scrubs frantically at her ear.*)

JULIE: Yak! Yak! Yak!

TIM: What? What's wrong?

(*Still scrubbing, JULIE gets to her feet and dances away.*)

JULIE: Yak, yak, yak, yak, yak, yak, yak....

URSULA: What happened?

LILITH: He stuck his tongue in her ear

(*They all look at TIM in disgust.*)

TIM: What? That's what they do! I saw it in a film!

JULIE: Yak, bloody yak –

TIM: Shut up. Your ear tasted funny anyway. Like – mustard.

JULIE: Mustard?

(*They all laugh.*)

PETER: What shall we play now?

URSULA: I'm still on. One, mississippi, two mississippi…

(*They all run to a door, then turn and level their gazes at the audience, before spinning the doors back to the warehouse side.*)

Scene 7

They push the doors out to the edges of the stage area, then turn and walk into the warehouse. They are all edgy, discreetly looking at their watches.

TIM: (*To JULIE – encouraging.*) Not long now.

(*She nods. Another pause. She strides over and picks up the book.*)

JULIE: We might as well finish it.

(*She begins to read and as she reads, the forest music begins to play. PETER, TIM, URSULA and LILITH move upstage and stand in a line with their backs to the audience. As JULIE tells the story, they turn and walk slowly downstage, taking on the roles of HANSEL and GRETEL but in a stylised, synchronised way.*)

Hansel and Gretel walked deeper and deeper into the forest. The trees were so tall and so close together, they made a dark roof which kept out all the sunlight. The wind moaned and the trees sighed and the two children hurried on, holding hands and never, ever looking behind them. Finally, when they were so light-headed with tiredness and hunger, they thought they might simply float away, they came to a clearing in the forest where sunlight poured down like melted butter.

(*The four are downstage now. They react, seeing the little house in front of them.*)

A little house nestled there and, as they got closer, they saw that the roof was made of pancakes and the walls were made of pies. They fell on the house and ate and ate and ate. And all the while, hidden inside, the witch was waiting.

(*Instantly the expressions of delight on their faces disappear. All four of them are now the witch.*)

She had been waiting for hours with all her knives sharpened and her oven hot. You see witches have weak, red eyes and cannot see very far, but they have a fine sense of smelling –

(*They all take a deep breath in, then turn and walk back upstage, slowly.*)

– and she had caught the scent of tender children when they were still a long way off. On that day, the witch was a woman, an old woman called Baba Yaga, but a witch has many names and many disguises. As anyone familiar with witches knows, the only way to spot one is to look for what is missing.

(*TIM stops, turning to face the audience.*)

Witches are always incomplete.

(*URSULA stops and turns.*)

And they yearn for the thing they have lost.

(*PETER stops and turns.*)

That is why they have such a hunger to fill themselves.

(*LILITH stops and turns.*)

Baba Yaga watched the children through her sugarpane window and saw their chubby, red cheeks and the saliva sprang into her mouth. And she said:

EVERYONE: That will be a good bite!

(*JULIE slams the book shut and they all turn their heads*

sharply to stare at LILITH. Suddenly unsure of herself,
LILITH moves downstage and begins fussing with a line
of cut-out dolls. URSULA, PETER and JULIE exit.
TIM stays.)

Scene 8

LILITH fusses with the cut-out dolls. TIM watches.

TIM: No wonder you went into catering. You're really good at
stirring things.

LILITH: I beg your pardon –

TIM: Oh, come on! Ever since you got here.

LILITH: What are you talking about – ?

TIM: A little stir here, a little shake there. And then – your
chef's special.

LILITH: How many pints did you have?

TIM: You already had them at each other's throats. Why the
name thing too?

LILITH: Clearwater. It's a ridiculous name!

TIM: All right. Let's talk about another name. Let's talk about
James.

(A pause. LILITH turns her back on TIM and moves up-
stage, holding up her cut-out dolls against one of the doors.)

LILITH: I think we need something here. Don't you?

TIM: That photograph you showed me. I've seen it before.

LILITH: Yes? No? Another colour?

TIM: I was doing a job across town a couple of months ago. A
loft conversion?

(LILITH pauses for an instant, giving TIM one, anguished
glance, then returning to her fussing.)

That's where I've seen it before. The photograph. They
had a larger print of it. Framed. Hanging in their hallway.

LILITH: It's a school photo! They all look the same.

TIM: Not that one. See, I recognised the uniform. That used
to be my Alice's school. The boy in the photo – he even
wears his tie the same way she did. A bit rebellious, you
know? Loose. Crooked. Big fat knot to it.

LILITH: Red, I think.

TIM: Nice lad. What was his name? Daniel. That was it. Daniel.

(*LILITH gives up any pretence of working. She turns round and waits for TIM to say what he has to say.*)

His mother was telling me about Daniel's auntie. She wouldn't leave the boy alone. When they tried to cut down the visits, she came over and picked him off the street where he was playing. Took him away for a whole week end.

LILITH: We went to the seaside. He was fine!

TIM: What's going on here, Lilith?

LILITH: Nothing! Nothing's going on, Tim. Just leave it.

TIM: If he's Daniel, why the hell are you calling him James?

LILITH: James was mine! My baby. My James. He would be six now, the same age as Daniel. I look at Daniel and I see James. Not all the time, just every now and then. My James. Looking back at me.

(*Behind the doors, the other three actors sing a wordless melody, a call and answer which starts very simply and gradually grows in complexity. As LILITH talks, she keeps stopping, as though listening to the melody. She makes a rhythm, her voice and the music, like two beating hearts. She may even sing, the 'to and fro' lines.*)

There's a song, you see… A song… I never knew… Until he was born – that's when it starts. To – and fro – to – and fro… It comes from deep inside. And it tugs. It tugs. He sings his first notes. And you answer. You answer. And you add more notes and the tune grows as he grows. And it builds. It builds. To and fro, to and fro –

(*The wordless melody stops. There is a pause.*)

And then his song stopped. He was only two weeks old. His song stopped. And I so wanted to hear the rest of it. I so want to hear it…

(*A pause as LILITH shakes off the memories and comes back to the warehouse.*)

I tried to keep him safe. I couldn't. My little lost boy. You know…?

TIM: I know.

LILITH: I don't think you do.

TIM: Lilith, they won't let you near Daniel again, no matter how many floats you build.

LILITH: Oh, yes! So – reasonable! None of you know what it's like.

TIM: I know you can't go around creating misery just because you're miserable –

LILITH: So reasonable! You've all still got your children!
(*A pause.*)

TIM: Alice didn't come to see me last week. Or the week before. She had something on. With her friends. You know? The last time she visited, she didn't even want to watch Buffy any more. 'Dad, that's so – last century…' It's a different song now. You know?

LILITH: I know. I'm sorry. I should go.

TIM: Stay. We could go for a drink after. I can tell you about the motorbike trip I'm planning for this summer. I've got the time now. Besides, we have to wait. Make sure Sean comes back safe. He should be –
(*TIM stops to look at his watch and JULIE, PETER and URSULA enter simultaneously.*)

EVERYONE: – back by now…
(*They look out towards the dark wasteground. An owl hoots. They look up, then move over to the doors and spin them to the mirrored side.*)

Scene 9

The owl hoots again. They all look up, children now. There is the glow of a small camp fire downstage centre. The five move slowly towards the fire, looking for kindling as they go. They are dreamy with tiredness and sun. Again, they are each in their own world but their sounds and movements weave together in a bigger pattern as they converge.

JULIE: (*Twirling at each repeat of the line and bringing each door in to make a semi-circle around the fire.*) Star light, star bright, first star I see tonight… Star light, star bright, first star I see tonight… (*Continuing.*)
(*PETER and LILITH move carefully through the jungle, now and again dropping to one knee and using the sticks under their arms like sub-machine guns – with sound*

118

effects. TIM is indulging in short bursts of sword fighting with his stick. URSULA is pretending to ski with her two sticks.)

URSULA: Shooop, shooop...

(*One by one, they add their kindling to the fire and sit down, leaning against one another unselfconsciously. PETER gets out a pen knife and begins stripping the bark from a small branch.*)

This has been a great island.

JULIE: Shall we come back tomorrow?

TIM: We could stay here all night.

LILITH: Yeah! We could make ourselves little nests out of leaves and grass and stuff.

URSULA: The fire will keep us warm.

JULIE: And we could cook a meal on it.

TIM: What would we eat?

LILITH: We could make soup out of leaves and grass and stuff.

JULIE: If we dug, we might find potatoes.

(*PETER holds up his sharpened stick.*)

PETER: I could spear a fish in the river. (*He holds up his knife as well.*) Or, I could kill a rabbit!

TIM: You couldn't.

PETER: I could. I'd find a burrow and wait for it. They come out at dusk.

TIM: It's past dusk now, stupid.

URSULA: Yeah (*She looks around with the beginnings of unease.*) It's night now, nearly.

(*The owl hoots. They pause to listen.*)

PETER: And when I catch it, I'll kill it with my knife.

LILITH: Poor little rabbit.

PETER: And I'll pull all its skin off and pull all its guts out.

LILITH: Shut u–up!

PETER: Then I'll poke this stick through it and cook it on the fire.

JULIE: Yak! I'm not eating that!

URSULA: You would if you were starving.

JULIE: I wouldn't.

TIM: I would. I'd eat all the meat 'til there was nothing left but a raw head and bloody bones.

JULIE: And if you did, its ghost would come in the dark to pay you back. And it would be ten times as big. And you would hear it coming because it would swing its raw head from side to side and the grass would go swish, swish.

LILITH: And it would come up behind you with its bloody bones clacking together. And it would grab you and then it would eat you –

URSULA: Don't say that!

JULIE: You're not scared, are you?

URSULA: No! Are you?

JULIE: No. I used to be scared. But I'm not now.

(*The owl hoots. They stop to listen.*)

PETER: Everyone say one thing you used to be scared of.

JULIE: Clowns.

URSULA: Things in museums.

TIM: Father Christmas.

LILITH: Old people.

PETER: Monsters.

JULIE: Yeah, monsters.

URSULA: Monsters still scare me –

PETER: Shhhhh! We said it three times! They can come and find us now!

(*They are suddenly scared for real. Throughout the next few exchanges, they become increasingly frightened, drawing nearer to the fire and to each other.*)

JULIE: There's something moving – over by the old warehouse. Look.

URSULA: But they won't come here, will they? The fire will keep them away, won't it?

(*They all add their sticks to the fire.*)

TIM: There's a monster under the railway bridge over there. Right up in the roof bit, behind the big girder. It's got yellow eyes and sometimes it sings. You can tell when it's there, because it slavers and the slaver runs down the wall. That's when you have to keep looking behind you. It catches people who don't look behind them.

URSULA: In the park, in the trees behind the swings, there's a monster. It looks quite a lot like a man, but if you go into the trees on your own, it will open its mouth wide, like a snake, and it will swallow you. A little boy went in there after his ball one time and he never came out again.

JULIE: There's one in my room. Under my bed. It's asleep most of the time but sometimes it wakes up in the middle of the night. It's slimy and pale and has grey fluff stuck all over it. It used to have eyes but it stayed in the dark under my bed so long the skin grew over them. But it can still smell me.

(*JULIE breathes in through her nose – a long breath – imitating the way the monster tests the air. They all nod in complete understanding.*)

It can sniff me out. And it's got shears.

LILITH: But the worst one of all is the bogeyman –

TIM: Shhhhh!

(*TIM shakes his head and puts his hands over LILITH's mouth, fumbling, gentle – a reminder not to voice the monster rather than a physical gagging. They are all now seeing their own personal worst monster. LILITH pulls TIM's hands away.*)

LILITH: But it's the bogeyman –

TIM/JULIE/PETER/URSULA: Shhhh…

(*TIM again puts his hands gently to LILITH's mouth, and the others also either put their hands to LILITH's face or cover their own mouths. TIM nods and LILITH nods back to him, her eyes wide above his hands. The others nod too. It is a moment filled with intense fear and it is at this moment that the fire begins to die down. They turn and stare at it in horror. PETER attempts to poke it back to life, which puts it out. They pull together in a tight knot, holding hands, backs together, each facing outwards and trying to look everywhere at once. They are all tearful, on the edge of panic. It is JULIE who starts the chant, in a shaking, faltering voice.*)

JULIE: …moonlight…starlight… The bogeyman's not out tonight… Moonlight, starlight, the bogeyman's NOT out tonight.

(JULIE continues the chant and, one by one, the others join in. The chant grows in confidence and strength. They begin to stamp their feet to the rhythm of the words. Their chins come up. The fear leaves their faces. The chanting and the stamping grow louder and louder until the final repetition is at full volume.)

ALL: Moonlight! Starlight! The bogey man's *NOT* out tonight!

(A pause. A silence.)

TIM: I'm bored with this game. Let's go home!

(They cheer and scatter in all directions calling goodbyes and see-you-tomorrows as they go. They stop at the doors, their backs to the audience. The owl hoots. They look over their shoulders, then send a level stare into the audience. They spin the doors to the warehouse side, disappearing behind the doors as they do so.)

Scene 10

The stage darkens. For a moment, it remains dark and empty. The wind rises, the sound adding to the desolation. The five adults enter, each carrying a torch. They are searching for Sean. The torch beams sweep the audience, zig zagging through the dark as the five search, calling Sean's name. The lights come up. In silence, they move downstage, clicking off their torches. They are silent for a moment, then they all start talking, attempting to reassure JULIE and themselves. PETER, in contrast, is pessimistic.

TIM: He'll be back.

PETER: He's late.

LILITH: Barely –

URSULA: Barely –

PETER: Late.

JULIE: Not that late – *(A pause.)* He'll be through that door in a minute.

URSULA: Surprised at all the fuss –

TIM: Mu-u-um! Get o-o-ff!

PETER: But he's late.

LILITH: Not that late…

(A pause. Then JULIE can't pretend any more.)

JULIE: Where is he?

PETER: I warned you.

JULIE: Where's my Sean?

PETER: I told you.

JULIE: Some monster's got him!

PETER: Yes…

URSULA: No!

(*A pause, then LILITH voices their thoughts.*)

LILITH: Perhaps we should – maybe it's time to call the
police?

PETER: Yes

URSULA: No! (*To JULIE.*) Give it a bit longer.

*(JULIE hesitates, then takes the mobile phone from her bag.
Instantly, the lights dim as the other four kneel in a line at
her feet, shining their torches up into her face, duplicating
television cameras and press flashbulbs. JULIE begins to
speak, upset but trying to keep control of herself, as though
she is at a press conference.)*

JULIE: Please. If anyone saw anything. Please He's only nine.
He was wearing green combat pants, a black Taz T-shirt,
and blue and white trainers. Please… if you saw anything… He's small for his age. There's a chip out of his left
front tooth. His hair is – always messy. He never finishes
his drinks. He's ticklish. He sleeps with his head under the
pillow. He can balance a tennis ball on his nose… Please, if
you saw anything –

*(Suddenly, URSULA jumps to her feet and turns to face the
audience. The lights come back up and the others turn off
their torches. URSULA brings them back to the warehouse.)*

URSULA: No. We do that and we're in a different place. He's
really missing then. (*She indicates the black and white headline
house behind them.*) We built that. We made it.

(JULIE looks around her, beginning to understand.)

Moonlight, starlight. The bogeyman's not out tonight.

*(URSULA nods at the others, encouraging them to join
in. JULIE stands and joins her in the chant, then TIM,
then LILITH and, finally, PETER. They get louder and
louder, stamping their feet, until they are shouting and the
floor is trembling. They move towards the black and white*

headline house and position themselves in a line in front of it, their backs to the audience.)

ALL: Moonlight! Starlight! The bogeyman's not out tonight!
(*They rip down the headline house, revealing a colourful child's painting house underneath.*)

Scene 11

JULIE turns and runs back upstage, looking around expectantly for Sean. A long moment as the others slowly join her and hope fades. Then JULIE's mobile phone, still in her hand, begins to ring. She stares at it, not wanting to answer. Not wanting to know. Finally she accepts the call.

JULIE: Hello…?
(*Everyone waits. JULIE listens. Her face crumples. She ends the call.*)

URSULA: Julie…?

JULIE: He's safe.
(*URSULA hugs JULIE.*)
He went home. The little bugger went home. I'll bloody kill him!
(*URSULA backs away and, suddenly, JULIE and PETER are facing one another. PETER is unsure of himself. JULIE gives him a cool stare.*)

PETER: I'm – glad.

JULIE: Yeah?

PETER: About the wasteground. I should have said earlier. Go down to the council offices. You've still got time to put in an objection –

JULIE: Doesn't matter. The kids'll find somewhere else. They always do. So. Go ahead. Build your – complex.

PETER: Not me. I only build houses. (*Although still ostensibly talking to JULIE, PETER is actually now talking to URSULA.*) I like making homes. For families. Somewhere for them to be together. Somewhere comfortable and safe.
(*URSULA is not the only one moved by this appeal. LILITH hears PETER talking about families and safety and she pulls the photograph of her nephew from her bag.*)

124

JULIE: I think I'll just… Head home…

URSULA: Go! Go…

(JULIE moves over to one of the five doors and stands facing it – effectively 'off-stage'. PETER and URSULA move together. TIM watches them then turns to LILITH.)

TIM: So. What about that drink?

(LILITH hesitates, looking down at the photograph.)

LILITH: I should get back…

TIM: You've got the time, you know.

(LILITH hesitates again. TIM watches her. She crumples the photograph into her fist then looks at TIM.)

LILITH: Yes. I know.

(They share a smile, then each goes to stand facing one of the doors. They are now 'off-stage'.)

URSULA: Shall we…?

PETER: What?

URSULA: Shall we start a new story?

PETER: What sort of story?

URSULA: One where all the good girls grow up, and the lost boys all come home.

(They stare at one another. URSULA smiles. PETER hesitates, then smiles back and nods. URSULA moves up to PETER, cups his face in her hands and kisses him. The kiss is long and passionate.)

Come on. Let's go home.

PETER: I'll just…

(PETER indicates the torches etcetera, still scattered on the floor. URSULA nods and leaves. PETER collects up the torches, then notices the brass key lying upstage in the corner. He picks up the key and the fairytale music starts to play. He takes off his watch, places it on the floor and kneels, preparing to smash it with the key. The others all turn to watch him. He is optimistic, hopeful, as he prepares to smash his watch, but he cannot bring himself to do it. The others turn back to the doors. The fairytale music is replaced by the memory/heartbeat music as, somewhere, a little boy starts crying in a tired, lost way. PETER, very controlled once more, straps his watch on again, picks up the key,

looks at the audience. He places the key in the middle of the floor, looks at the audience once more, then moves over to his door. In one, synchronised movement, they all turn the doors sharply, exiting behind them. The music cuts off. The key is left in the middle of the floor.)

The End.

Play out music: 'Stand By Me'; the Ben E. King version.

DEVIL'S GROUND

Note

The action takes place at the end of the sixteenth century in a robber valley in the Scottish Middle March. The glory days of the reivers were nearly over and the heroic, defiant rescue of Kinmont Willie from Carlisle Castle was perhaps their swansong. The imminent unification of the crowns under James as Elizabeth moved towards the end of her life meant that the great reiver riding families were becoming an embarrassment to the authorities. Their bravery and their violent nature, which were once welcome assets on the border, now made them a dangerous liability, but they knew no other way of life and did not know how to change. The authorities began to come down hard on the reiver families, who responded with increasing violence and with fighting amongst themselves to settle old scores. They knew their time was nearly over. In 1603, Elizabeth died. James abolished Border laws and Wardens and instituted the systematic destruction of the reivers, demolishing their strongholds, executing them in their hundreds, confiscating their land and banishing many of the great Names.

Characters

JENNET
the Laird's wife. In her late thirties

MICHAEL
the Laird. In his mid-forties. His father was William,
the Devil o' the Moss

CLEM
in his early twenties. The last surviving son
of Jennet and Michael

THOMAS
in his early twenties. A member of the enemy family living
in the household as a pledge, or hostage. An asthmatic with
a weak heart

MARGARET
the Laird's mother. In her early sixties

Devil's Ground was first performed at Victoria Halls, Selkirk on 17 October 2002, with the following cast:

JENNET, Siobhan Brough

MICHAEL, Stewart Howson

CLEM, Paul McDonald

THOMAS, Graham Vernall

MARGARET, Alison Coates

Director, Gillian Hambleton

Designer, Cath Young

Stage Manager, Richard Jarvis

ACT ONE

Scene 1

The stage is in semi-darkness. The lighting, blue-green with an underwater feel, shows the darkened, night-quiet main hall of a pele. The set is stylised. Furnishings are minimal, but must include a kist (storage box or basket), a jug and a pitcher. Athough other items of furniture may serve as seats, there is only one chair, the Laird's chair. A sword, shield and dagger are on display, alongside a filthy, tattered standard and a lance. They are arranged with care and are obviously of some importance. To one side, there is a curtained bed. The curtains are sheer, muslin or similar, but the area they enclose should be treated as a separate bed-chamber. A window is delineated by the rectangle of moonlight that marks the floor, dissected into squares by an iron window grille. This window looks out on the Devil's Ground. Directly below the window is the drowning hole. At each side of the stage, two or three long, thin lengths of material hang from the rigging to the floor, one behind the other. The material is blue with faint outlines of reivers on horse-back, or similar war-like images, sketched on them. They look like banners or flags of some sort. They act as places for people to eavesdrop, or to conceal themselves, as at the end of the play.

JENNET is slumped in the Laird's chair, asleep. She has spent a fitful night waiting for her husband MICHAEL and her son CLEM to return from a raid. She is dressed in a white shift and has a long length of blue-green silk wrapped around her shoulders.

A jagged, frightening sequence of notes or sound effects (referred to from now on as the Devil's Music) begins to play. JENNET becomes agitated in her sleep as her nightmare builds. A figure appears, wearing reiver armour, a steel helmet and a cloak. It carries a sword and a tattered banner identical to the items displayed. There is no face beneath the helmet, only a skull. The figure looms over JENNET and lowers the tattered standard onto her face. She chokes and gasps for breath as though drowning. The figure turns, raises the sword and standard and roars out a battle cry.

FIGURE: To the Devil!

(*JENNET starts awake, gasping for air. She cries out as the figure turns back to her. Curling up in the chair, she hides her face. The figure exits as THOMAS hurries onstage, wrapped in a blanket. The Devil's Music stops. JENNET uncurls and lifts her head. She sees THOMAS and cries out again, jumping from the chair and running to the window. As she runs, the long length of blue-green silk trails out behind her before finally dropping from her shoulders. JENNET turns and then relaxes as she recognises THOMAS.*)

JENNET: Thomas!

THOMAS: Aye.

JENNET: I thought you were…

(*JENNET searches behind THOMAS, looking for the apparition but seeing nothing.*)

THOMAS: Who?

JENNET: (*Embarrassment vying with fear.*) The old Laird.

THOMAS: The Devil o' the Moss?

(*He lifts his shift to knee height, displaying his skinny legs.*) Me?

(*JENNET does not laugh.*)

JENNET: I saw him.

THOMAS: You were dreaming.

JENNET: Aye… But his face was a skull –

THOMAS: Then how did you ken who it was?

JENNET: The banner. It was his.

THOMAS: Then death has made him awful neat.

(*JENNET looks puzzled. THOMAS points to the banner.*) He put it back before he left. (*JENNET laughs.*) It was a dream.

JENNET: Aye. A dream. But – he gave the rallying cry. Did you hear?

THOMAS: No. How could I? You were –

JENNET: – dreaming.

(*JENNET smiles, finally convinced.*)

THOMAS: Even he cannae rise from the dead. He's out there, buried deep in the Devil's Ground.

(*JENNET shivers.*)

THOMAS: (*Unreadable.*) And you will soon join him.

JENNET: (*Startled.*) What…?

THOMAS: …you're shivering with cold. Here…

(*THOMAS picks up the length of silk and wraps it around her shoulders. He rubs the edge of the silk between his fingers.*)

Such fine cloth.

JENNET: (*Proudly.*) Silk.

THOMAS: (*Gently teasing.*) Oh. Silk.

JENNET: A gift from Michael. A wedding gift.

THOMAS: Just the thing for a Borders winter.

JENNET: It was a love gift, Thomas! Sense didnae come intae it. He thought it would make a pretty gown, but I couldnae bear to cut such cloth. Left like this, it could still be anything.

THOMAS: Except warm. I'll close the shutters.

JENNET: No. Don't shut us in. Not yet.

THOMAS: Lady, any watcher would be forgiven for thinking you the prisoner here.

JENNET: I – couldnae breathe, in my…

THOMAS: Dream?

JENNET: I was drowning. Weeds and slime in my mouth. Filthy black water over my head –

(*JENNET turns to the window and looks down. Greenish light from the drowning hole dapples her face.*)

I was down there. In his drowning hole…

THOMAS: Not a drowning hole. Not now. He isnae here to use it. Now it is a peat hag like any other.

JENNET: Like any other? (*She shakes her head.*) Too many have died in it for that. And still I cannae breathe…

THOMAS: It is the cold air –

JENNET: No! There is no air here.

THOMAS: (*Pulling his blanket tighter about him against the icy breeze pouring in through the unglazed window.*) There is plenty ower here.

(*Throughout the following description, JENNET demonstrates with her hands as she talks, starting with her fists clenched together in a ball, then moving her hands out to suggest each successive barrier.*)

JENNET: Inside this tower – the bogs, the forest – then such deep valley sides –

THOMAS: This valley is a stronghold, Lady, for you and all your name. My family has often had cause to curse it.

JENNET: A stronghold. Thomas, if I could choose, I wouldnae live in a stronghold. Especially here. This pele is built on –

THOMAS: Evil ground. The old tales again, is it?

JENNET: One of Cloutie's Crofts. (*She makes the sign of the cross.*) Land never ploughed, left as a tithe for the Devil –

THOMAS: (*Laughing.*) Then the Devil gets a poor deal. Stinking bogs and peat hags! It is not ploughed because nothing would grow there. That is all.

JENNET: But the tales… Fetches and faery folk…

(*THOMAS picks up his fiddle and tunes it as he talks, then plucks a few notes.*)

THOMAS: The tales are why the Devil o' the Moss built here. He was a clever man, your father-in-law. He knew folk would fear him if he claimed the Devil's Ground for his own. No doubt he fed the whispers that something worse than Jeddart staffs defended his walls.

JENNET: Do you fear nothing, Thomas?

THOMAS: Plenty. But my fears are all in this world.

JENNET: These last few months. I have felt. I have thought…

THOMAS: What?

JENNET: Something is walking in the Devil's Ground. It grows stronger every day.

(*THOMAS carefully lays down the fiddle.*)

THOMAS: Lady. Do not fear the tales. Look to your own family.

(*JENNET draws herself up to her full height and destroys the closeness they have built between them.*)

JENNET: You forget your place, pledge!

(*THOMAS bows.*)

THOMAS: Then I shall return to my chamber.

JENNET: How did you get out?

THOMAS: The Laird left my door unbarred.

JENNET: He forgot?

THOMAS: Your husband has left my door unbarred every
   night these two weeks past.
   (*JENNET looks shocked, then recovers herself.*)
JENNET: Then he has grown to trust you, I think.
THOMAS: No. He is hoping I might escape.
JENNET: (*Putting her hands to her belly.*) Michael cannae want
   such a thing.
THOMAS: Lady, look at me! What do you see? I would have
   died years ago but for my mother's nursing. I would have
   died here but for your herbs and medicines. I cannae ride.
   I cannae fight. Fight! I'm too busy fighting for air! What
   use is a man whose chest closes up like a fist whenever it
   chooses? No use at all. I'm useless.
JENNET: You are not! You lift a grand tune from a fiddle –
   and you can wheedle a duck off a tarn.
THOMAS: Music and words. What use in these times? Jennet.
   Do you ken what I am saying? The life of a pledge must be
   worth something. My brothers do not value my life.
JENNET: Oh, Thomas, your brothers –
THOMAS: Will never give themselves up to the Warden. Not
   for me.
JENNET: A year and a day. It was agreed. There is still a little
   time left.
THOMAS: They will not give themselves up. My life will
   be forfeit. My life for the life of the Devil o' the Moss?
   Your Laird sees that as a poor exchange. If the law cannae
   deliver his father's killers –
JENNET: Michael gave his word to the Warden.
THOMAS: And now he wants me to untie his hands. If I try
   to escape before the year is up, your Laird can kill me and
   then ride against my brothers with his conscience clear.
JENNET: And will you try?
THOMAS: No. Only those of your name know the safe paths
   through the bogs. And every man in this valley has a slue-
   dog to track me and a sturdy Galloway to ride me down.
   I'll stay. That way, I'll be warm and dry when I die.
JENNET: There must be another way. I will talk to Michael
   when he returns.

THOMAS: Best left, Lady. Call trouble by name and it lifts its head.

(*A figure appears silently behind them, but THOMAS and JENNET do not notice. MARGARET stays in the shadows, listening.*)

THOMAS: It is a reiver's moon tonight.

JENNET: (*Anxious.*) Aye. Michael rides.

THOMAS: Where does he ride?

JENNET: He –

MARGARET: (*Striding into the room.*) Enough!

JENNET: But, I only –

MARGARET: You are my son's wife! You do not feed him to his enemies!

JENNET: Thomas is not –

MARGARET: – our enemy? If you think him a friend, you are a fool. His loyalty is to his name, as yours is to ours. Even now, he may be spying for his murderous brothers.

THOMAS: Am I a spy, witch? Can't you tell?

JENNET: Thomas!

MARGARET: Be careful, pledge –

THOMAS: Tell me, witch. They say you can keek into folk's heads, into secret places, even into the future. Do your spells not tell you what I am? Or is it only keyholes you can keek through?

MARGARET: You – ! I need no spells to ken your future. It is awful short, pledge. And it ends in death.

(*To JENNET.*) And you! Out here, half dressed, with him!

JENNET: Thomas heard me cry out. I fell asleep waiting for Michael and I dreamed I saw…

(*JENNET glances at the banner and weapons. MARGARET notices.*)

I had a bad dream.

MARGARET: So. You have seen him. (*She notes JENNET's fearful reaction and sees that she has hit the mark.*) I knew it.

JENNET: You knew…?

THOMAS: (*To JENNET.*) Ach! She didnae –

MARGARET: (*To JENNET, overriding THOMAS.*) I knew he would walk. How can the Devil o'the Moss rest, with his death unavenged?

THOMAS: She guessed, that's all! She saw, just now, when you looked towards his standard.

JENNET: It was a dream –

MARGARET: No. No dream. He will walk again. He will find a way to follow the blood feud –

JENNET: No...

MARGARET: He will choose the weakest of us. He will take the weakest –

JENNET: No!

(MARGARET watches JENNET's distress with satisfaction until THOMAS steps in front of her.)

THOMAS: I see what you are doing. I see you.

(MARGARET and THOMAS square up to one another. Off-stage, MICHAEL returns from the raid, shouting, exhilarated.)

MICHAEL: *(Off.)* Tam! Where is the lad? Look at them, Clem! Fine wee horses!

JENNET: They are home!

Scene 2

MARGARET continues to glare at THOMAS until the instant when MICHAEL and CLEM make their entrance.

MICHAEL: Jennet?

JENNET: Here! A good night?

MICHAEL: A charmed night. Seven good horses and eighty head of fine Cumberland cattle –

MARGARET: Whisht!

(MARGARET nods her head towards THOMAS but MICHAEL only laughs.)

MICHAEL: The lad's harmless, mother! *(Looking at THOMAS with some exasperation.)* He seems to like it here.

CLEM: That doesnae surprise me.

(CLEM and THOMAS glare.)

JENNET: *(To MICHAEL.)* And none were hurt?

(Throughout the following conversation, MICHAEL and CLEM begin to take off their armour and outer clothes. MICHAEL hands his things to JENNET. CLEM is still

glaring at THOMAS but MARGARET steps between them and gives CLEM a warning look before helping him with his armour.)

MICHAEL: Andrew's Jock came home tied across his saddle.

JENNET: Killed?

MICHAEL: Sleeping.

JENNET: Sleeping?

MICHAEL: (*Laughing.*) Like a bairn.

JENNET: Was he sick?

MICHAEL: Love-sick.

JENNET: Andrew's Jock? Never!

MICHAEL: Aye. And he couldnae bear to leave her behind.

JENNET: He took a lassie on a raid?

MICHAEL: A lassie…

(MICHAEL leans against CLEM, laughing. CLEM moves away.)

JENNET: If you willnae talk sense, I'm away to my bed.

MICHAEL: Jennet, come back! I'll tell you.

JENNET: Well?

MICHAEL: It was the little mare he brought.

JENNET: The grey that won him the bell at the last races?

MICHAEL: He willnae ride any other since then. But that mare, she's no good on a raid. Too flighty. She threw him on his head as we rode down on the herd. Out like a candle!

JENNET: No trouble, then? No hot trod?

MICHAEL: There shouldha been, what with the mare whinnying and Jock snoring, and the sound carrying clear and far in the frost. But not a soul stirred. (*MICHAEL becomes quieter, thinking about the implications of their charmed night.*) It was quiet at the ford, too.

MARGARET: What? No Warden's watch?

CLEM: Aye, but only four men. Three were all for turning their backs and pissing in the bushes as we went by – but the young one, he called a challenge.

MICHAEL: He was a brave lad.

CLEM: Brave? He was stupid.

JENNET: Clem, you didnae…

CLEM: I had to take him.

JENNET: But, just a lad? How old?

CLEM: Old enough.

MICHAEL: (*Amused, not seeing JENNET's stricken look.*) Though his sword was meant for a bigger man.

(*MICHAEL picks up his sword and imitates the boy, staggering backwards as he tries to swing it around his head. CLEM smiles as he watches JENNET's distress. THOMAS shows his disgust and MARGARET glares at him. MICHAEL, still clowning, falls backwards. Quickly, CLEM lunges forward and holds his sword at his father's throat. For a few seconds CLEM savours the power of his position, then MICHAEL frowns, pushes the sword aside and rises to his feet.*)

What did he call out, the lad, as you finished him?

CLEM: (*Bored, polishing his sword with his shirt-tail.*) 'Mother,' I think... Aye. (*Turning to JENNET, with venom.*) He called for his mother.

(*JENNET winces and, once again, brings her hands protectively to her belly. THOMAS sees the action and understands that JENNET is pregnant. MICHAEL and CLEM notice nothing, MICHAEL is still trying to pin down his growing unease over the events of the night.*)

MICHAEL: No, no. He said something before that. You didnae hear it?

(*CLEM shrugs, but MARGARET is picking up on MICHAEL's unease.*)

'You next,' he said. 'They'll have you next.' What did the lad mean?

CLEM: Ach! He was nothing. A skinny wee farmer's get with his arse hanging out of his breeks.

THOMAS: And you killed him.

(*CLEM turns to stare at THOMAS.*)

A brave deed. A deed to match the rescue of Kinmont Willie. They'll sing of you in ballads, with all the other heroes.

(*THOMAS begins to mock CLEM by singing The Ballad of Kinmont Willie. His singing runs beneath all the other dialogue and a 'duel' develops between THOMAS and CLEM as CLEM responds to THOMAS's mockery with increasingly graphic descriptions of the violence at the ford.*)

CLEM: (*Slowly, moving towards THOMAS.*) He was trying to run, when I killed him. He had his back to me. I drove my lance in between his shoulder blades and out through his belly. I pinned him to the river bed until he stopped twitching. His guts unraveled in the water.

(*JENNET turns away from her son, distraught. THOMAS continues to sing. MARGARET watches, pleased to see CLEM's anger. She needs him to be angry.*)

MICHAEL: It was work to be done. That's all.

MARGARET: And the other watchmen. What of them?

MICHAEL: Dealt with.

CLEM: (*Answering MARGARET but aimed at THOMAS, who is still singing.*) We drowned one in the river. Held him under and watched his face darken for lack of air. He took a while. The third, we crushed his head with a rock. Cracked his skull like an egg. Spilled his brains in the dirt. (*CLEM can stand the singing no longer. He goes for THOMAS, grabbing him around the throa…*)

I'll have you –

MICHAEL: Clem! He's not to be harmed. I gave my word!

(*CLEM keeps his hands around THOMAS's throat a moment longer, then lets go and stalks off-stage. JENNET turns on THOMAS.*)

JENNET: Are you wanting to die? Is that it? (*THOMAS shakes his head.*) Then why provoke him?

THOMAS: It is my only freedom.

MARGARET: (*To MICHAEL.*) And the fourth?

MICHAEL: (*Distracted.*) The fourth?

MARGARET: You said there were four watchmen at the ford.

MICHAEL: He ran.

MARGARET: Aye. And a man in fear of his life travels fast. He'll be telling his tale to the Warden before long…

MICHAEL: He wouldnae dare.

MARGARET: You shouldhae tracked him down. If your father was here –

MICHAEL: Well, he isnae!

(*MARGARET is silent. MICHAEL moves to placate her.*)

Eighty head in one night! The whole valley shall be fed this winter –

MARGARET: And your father's killers – (*Pointing at
THOMAS.*) – the pledge's brothers – lie easy in their beds. The
honour of our name is dying and you talk of filling larders.
MICHAEL: Times are changing. You must see –
MARGARET: I see a blood feud unsettled. I see a son who
looks out on his father's grave and takes no revenge!
Michael, for our name…for your father…for me…
MICHAEL: Mother, I gave my word.
(*MARGARET stalks off-stage.*)

Scene 3

*MICHAEL flings himself into the Laird's chair and scowls down
at his boots. The chair should be a symbol of his power, but he does
not look comfortable or sure of himself. In the silence, THOMAS
and JENNET share a look. THOMAS picks up his fiddle and
bow and tiptoes off-stage. JENNET moves over to her husband.
She strokes his hair and waits.*

MICHAEL: They named him the Devil o' the Moss. And
what name have I earned? The young laird. If I live to be
sixty, they will still call me the young laird.
JENNET: And how did your father earn his name?
MICHAEL: He was a strong laird –
JENNET: Ach! When he lived, all we planted were the bodies
of our sons. Fire was our harvest. Have you forgot the
famine so soon? Bairns eating grass to ease their bellies.
Women filling their cooking pots with snails for want of
any other meat. And all to serve the blood feud.
MICHAEL: Yet they followed him without question –
JENNET: None would dare question! If they did, they died
out there, in the filthy water of his drowning hole. Red and
black were his colours. You have brought us green and
gold again. You let the harvest grow.
MICHAEL: By doing nothing!
JENNET: You went to the Warden. You accepted Thomas as
a pledge –
(*MICHAEL makes a dismissive noise.*)
You stopped the blood feud. Someone had tae.

MICHAEL: And the honour of our name?

JENNET: What use honour when the name is gone? All but one of our sons lie in the Devil's Ground. And Clem. Since John was killed –

MICHAEL: No. Don't start on that again.

JENNET: But he –

MICHAEL: I said no!

JENNET: Aye. Well. Maybe he'll grow right again, now you have given us peace. He might. Folk must have peace to grow right, the same as harvests.

(Again JENNET cups her hands to her belly. MICHAEL, still scowling at his boots, does not notice.)

MICHAEL: It is hard, Jennet. Mother of God, it is hard! Tonight's work is what I am trained for. I am no farmer.

JENNET: Aye. I know. But Michael – I have something to tell you.

MICHAEL: Can't it wait?

JENNET: Until the summer. Then nothing will stop it.

MICHAEL: What?

JENNET: A bairn, Michael. I am to have a bairn.

(MICHAEL gets to his feet, delighted, incredulous.)

MICHAEL: Away! I thought we were past all that.

JENNET: Oh, I'm an old crone, right enough.

MICHAEL: No! I only meant – after all this time…

JENNET: Aye. I know. I thought so too. But –

MICHAEL: But –

(JENNET laughs. MICHAEL laughs too, then moves around the room, emotional, not quite knowing what to do with himself.)

JENNET: Well…?

(MICHAEL returns to JENNET and puts his hand on her belly.)

MICHAEL: Well. Well…

(They embrace. The embrace becomes sexual, intense. Off-stage, THOMAS begins to play a haunting, traditional melody. MICHAEL shakes his head and breaks away.)

He's like a lassie, that one.

JENNET: He is not!

MICHAEL: Skreeking wee tunes –

JENNET: Tunes you have sung to!

142

MICHAEL: Picking flowers –

JENNET: Herbs! And only to keep me company.

(*MICHAEL becomes serious.*)

MICHAEL: Now I've told you before. Dinnae grow ower-
fond of the lad.

JENNET: I cannae help it. He has a look of our own John
about him. His eyes.

(*MICHAEL lifts JENNET's chin, looking into her eyes.*)

MICHAEL: Your eyes…

(*They kiss. MICHAEL lifts a corner of the blue silk.*)

Remember our wedding night?

JENNET: Aye. Silk against our skin.

MICHAEL: You wrapped it around us…

(*JENNET loops a length of the material over his head, so
that it is wrapped around his shoulders as well as hers.*)

JENNET: Round and round… (*Another loop. They kiss again.*)

MICHAEL: And we stayed within its circle all night.

(*MICHAEL leads JENNET off-stage by pulling the silk
as THOMAS plays the last notes of his tune. As they exit,
MARGARET enters. She has been eavesdropping.*)

Scene 4

*MARGARET stares after MICHAEL and JENNET. The news of
a new baby has not pleased her. She moves across to the weapons,
reaches out and takes down the standard. Moving to look from the
window, she holds the cloth in her hand, running it through her
fingers, echoing MICHAEL and JENNET with the silk.*

MARGARET: I was awful grieved when he brought that silk
home. Do you remember? A waste, I told him. And you.
You laughed! There was no room in our lives for such
foolishness. No room. (*MARGARET pauses, shakes her head.*)
All the years it has lasted. Who wouldhae thought silk
could be sae strong…?

(*MARGARET grips the standard, her face full of bitterness,
envy, regret.*)

And now, there is to be a bairn. (*Holding up her hand as
though to forestall a protest.*)

143

I know. Bairns have never been the concern of the Devil o'
the Moss. But this could lose us the blood feud, do you
hear? After all we have been through…

(*MARGARET stops to regain control of herself.*)

It will make her stronger, this bairn. Michael willnae
avenge you, William. He will listen to her. A wee bit of
a bairn will make him shame our name. We shall have –
peace. And Clem! The name is nothing to him. He cares
only for –

(*MARGARET becomes still and the anger leaves her face
as an idea comes to her.*)

– himself…

(*MARGARET smiles. She turns, replaces the standard on
the wall and takes a pitcher, a bowl and a cloth from the
top of the kist.*)

Scene 5

*The light in the main hall of the pele brightens to daylight as
MARGARET carries the pitcher and bowl to the front of the stage.
CLEM wanders in, half dressed, yawning. She pours water into
the bowl and he washes his face. She hands him the drying cloth.
He finishes dressing, then goes to his jack, helmet and sword and
begins to put them on. Throughout all this, MARGARET is sizing
him up, judging her moment. At some point, she begins to talk.*

MARGARET: You ride today?

CLEM: Aye. There is black mail due.

MARGARET: Your father rides with you?

(*CLEM laughs.*)

CLEM: No. I do better alone.

MARGARET: So I have heard.

CLEM: (*Tense, suspicious.*) What have you heard?

MARGARET: They call you the Devil's get. They say you
show no mercy.

CLEM: (*Relaxing.*) That is how it must be. If they dinnae fear
me –

MARGARET: (*Correcting.*) Respect you.

CLEM: Aye. Respect. If they dinnae respect me, they willnae
pay the black mail.

144

MARGARET: That was William's way too. And the Laird?
Do they respect the Laird?

CLEM: My father *listens* to them. That is his way. He listens to
the greeting women and he takes what they offer, not what
we are due. One sack of barley instead of two, 'because
the crop was awful poor this year…' How can they respect
a Laird who wastes four hours in a game of football and
leaves, content, with the cart half empty?

(*MARGARET laughs, flattering him, then makes her
move.*)

MARGARET: When you ride, you have your own men to
command?

CLEM: Aye.

MARGARET: Always the same men?

CLEM: (*Warily.*) Aye.

MARGARET: Are they loyal to you?

CLEM: Without question.

MARGARET: And you could muster more?

CLEM: Why would I need tae?

MARGARET: Clem… Folk dinnae respect your father for
another reason –

(*She takes the sword from the display and holds it out to
him. CLEM suddenly realizes what his grandmother is
getting at. He holds up his hands and moves away from
her.*)

CLEM: Oh no. No. The blood feud is the Laird's business.

MARGARET: One night raid, Clem! One death to avenge
the Devil o'the Moss. Think of the reward.

CLEM: Reward?

MARGARET: The honour of our name restored.

CLEM: Oh that. I'll not go against my father.

MARGARET: You'd stand by and let him shame your name
by bowing to the Warden –

CLEM: It willnae come to that. He will fight – when he has
tae.

MARGARET: I wouldnae be so sure.

CLEM: Be careful what you say –

MARGARET: He listens to women. You said that yourself. He
listens to your mother and she makes him soft.

CLEM: Not that soft –

MARGARET: You think not? I warn you, soon the Laird may listen when she asks him to curb your…collecting methods. (*CLEM reacts with shock, realizing that MARGARET does know something about his business after all.*)

CLEM: He wouldnae listen…

MARGARET: No? She might even send him riding with you. How would you and your men fare then, hmmm? With every payment accounted for – every cartload coming home to the Devil's Ground?

CLEM: She doesnae have the power –

MARGARET: Not yet. But soon, soon she will. I have seen. (*CLEM stiffens. He has a strong superstitious streak and this side of MARGARET is something he fears.*)

CLEM: In the water? What have you seen?

MARGARET: She has news. For your father.

CLEM: What news?

MARGARET: It wasnae clear, when I looked –

CLEM: Try again! Look again! (*MARGARET leans over the bowl of water, staring intently at the surface. CLEM watches her. Neither of them notice that THOMAS has entered behind them.*)

MARGARET: Ah! I see it now.

CLEM: Tell me…

MARGARET: A bairn. Jennet is carrying a bairn. A new start, she tells the Laird. A new start made, an old feud gone. A peacable border, she tells him. No black mail –

CLEM: No black mail?

MARGARET: And a valley full of farmers.

CLEM: Farmers!

MARGARET: Aye. Muck and straw for your inheritance. And a brother to share it with. (*The news of a brother produces a reaction in CLEM which is deeper and more complex than the growing anger he has shown so far. Fear, resentment, anger, yes but something else too. MARGARET sees she has hit home without understanding why.*) Is that what you want? Another young brother after four years on your own? A brother like John, hmmm? That would please your mother –

146

CLEM: Is it a brother? Are you sure?

MARGARET: Aye. A brother.

THOMAS: Or a sister.

CLEM: You!

MARGARET: Spying, is it?

THOMAS: Plotting, is it?

(CLEM starts towards THOMAS but MARGARET stops him. THOMAS walks between them up to the bowl.)
Brother. Sister. She cannae tell you that. All she kens is that your mother is carrying a bairn and she didnae have to keek into the future for that! She found out the same way I did.

CLEM: What way?

THOMAS: By watching. Only watching. There's nothing to be seen in there – !
(THOMAS waves dismissively at the bowl, then stops and moves closer, staring at the water.)
Wait though –

CLEM: What?

THOMAS: I think I do see… Look! There!

MARGARET: I see nothing.

THOMAS: There. Move closer.
(MARGARET and CLEM lean over the bowl. THOMAS waits until they both have their faces close to the water.)
I see –
(THOMAS brings his hand down flat on the water in the bowl. MARGARET and CLEM both receive a faceful.)
– two fools!
(He laughs.)
You didnae see that in the water.
(CLEM grabs THOMAS by the back of the neck and forces his head down into the bowl. THOMAS struggles but CLEM holds him down. MARGARET does not try to intervene. CLEM lifts THOMAS's face clear of the water.)

CLEM: What do you see now, pledge?

THOMAS: …Nothing…

CLEM: Nothing? Then try again!
(Once again, he forces THOMAS's face down into the bowl and holds him there for a long moment. THOMAS's

struggles intensify, then weaken, then stop. CLEM lets go and THOMAS collapses to the floor. MARGARET calls to CLEM as he leaves the stage. He stops to listen but does not turn.)

MARGARET: Clem! We cannae turn away from the blood feud. If we do, where is our solid ground?

(*CLEM finishes his exit with MARGARET still calling after him.*)

We will flounder! We shall sink!

(*MARGARET turns to glare at THOMAS, curled on the floor. Then she too exits. THOMAS drags himself to his feet, coughing and choking. He leans over the bowl, propped on his hands. Reflected light shines up into his face. THOMAS becomes still. Suddenly he IS seeing something in the water. He reacts to the vision with horrified disbelief. The greenish underwater light spreads from the bowl as the lights dim until the dappled light fills the stage. THOMAS staggers away from the bowl as the Devil's Music starts to play. He stares out into the audience as his vision shows him what is coming to the valley. He turns upstage and attempts to run, but collapses in a corner, behind the Laird's chair.*)

Scene 6

The lighting returns to daylight as MICHAEL enters. He is not long out of bed and he has a rumpled look. He has pulled on some clothes but his shirt is open and he has a blanket for warmth. He is carrying the folded length of silk and he moves contentedly, the picture of a satisfied man. He rubs the silk against his face, smells it, then looks around, checking that he is alone. He does not see the unconscious THOMAS. Draping the silk over the Laird's chair, he strikes a pose and begins trying out names for his future son. His tone and demeanour should reflect the qualities he thinks are embodied in each name.

MICHAEL: Walter… No, no…

(*MICHAEL moves on, stops, tries another name.*)

Jock… Hmmm. Richard? James. Jamie! Jamie…?

(*He stops by his sword. Picks it up, examines it.*)

John…? Nay, she'll not have John. Not again.

(*He looks out over the Devil's Ground.*)
And she'd be right. Too much for the bairn to live up to.
And Clem – he'd take it wrong. He'd…
(*MICHAEL frowns, then closes off that line of thought.*)
Edward? (*He looks towards the tattered standard.*) William.
(*He lifts his sword, stares between the weapon and the standard.*)
Nay, father. He'll not be a William. He needs a name more
suited to the times. He'll be – (*He lets the sword drop.*)
– Michael.
(*MICHAEL turns, dragging the sword behind him, as
though he is ploughing a field.*)
Michael…
(*He turns, ploughs the next furrow.*)
Michael…
(*And the next furrow. He stops. He is struggling to accept a future
life which is foreign to him.*)
Michael.
(*He leans forward on his sword, resting his forehead on the
handle. THOMAS stirs and coughs. Quickly, MICHAEL
straightens up.*)

Scene 7

MICHAEL: Are you still here?
(*THOMAS's breathing is ragged and he is coughing.
MICHAEL is oblivious as he returns his sword to its place.*)
Come here. Come on! Over here.
(*MICHAEL manhandles THOMAS over to the window,
pointing to the Devil's Ground.*)
The frost lies heavy this morning. (*He looks at THOMAS and
continues, pointedly.*) Do you ken how it lies thickest on the
solid ground? See? The safe paths through the bog are clearly
marked. Anyone could walk them. Even in moonlight, they
would stand out. Do you ken what I say, pledge?
THOMAS: Aye.
MICHAEL: Well then.
(*MICHAEL slaps THOMAS on the back. His frustration
makes the action harder than he meant, nearly a blow.
THOMAS takes a few seconds to recover.*)

THOMAS: I shall not escape.

MICHAEL: Why?

THOMAS: Because the ground must be left in peace.

MICHAEL: Peace?

THOMAS: There is life curled under the frost. Growing things need peace.

MICHAEL: Peace and growth. Is that the way now?

THOMAS: The only way, I think. I have seen –

MICHAEL: Seen?

THOMAS: A vision –

MICHAEL: Away! Do I look like a kitchen crone? A ballad, now. I'd listen to a ballad. (*Laying his hand on the silk.*) A love song…

THOMAS: (*Coughing.*) I have nae voice for singing. I could tell a tale… (*MICHAEL nods.*) A Laird – let us call him James –

MICHAEL: – James, aye.

THOMAS: This Laird, his lands border on the lands of his cousin. Their two families have long been at feud and the Laird guards his border with fighting dogs. Then the Laird and his cousin – let us call her –

MICHAEL: (*Impatiently, well aware that he is getting a thinly disguised lesson on the national political situation of the day.*) – Elizabeth.

THOMAS: Aye. Elizabeth. James and Elizabeth, they make truce. Now James has no enemy to fight, but his dogs still roam the border, killing folk and taking beasts. This James, he starts thinking of leashes and muzzles. He starts thinking that his cousin is old –

MICHAEL: He starts thinking that she will die soon, leaving her land to him.

THOMAS: What will James do with his fighting dogs, then?

MICHAEL: Fighting dogs are no use for anything else.

THOMAS: But, what if the dogs change?

MICHAEL: Change?

THOMAS: To – to farm dogs. The Laird wouldnae turn against them then.

MICHAEL: Kings. This has always been the way with them.

When there are wars to be fought, we are their heroes. In peace time we are villains. He will turn again, James, the next time he needs us.

THOMAS: There willnae be a next time! When Elizabeth dies – no more border. No more dogs.

MICHAEL: So, the king and my wife are in agreement. They would both have me be a farmer. (*He looks at THOMAS suspiciously.*) Did she tell you to say these things?

THOMAS: No.

MICHAEL: Then, do you argue for your life, pledge?

THOMAS: No. (*Looking to the bowl.*) My life will end soon whether you take it or not –

(*THOMAS halts as JENNET enters and MICHAEL stops listening.*)

MICHAEL: Jennet!

(*MICHAEL guides her to the Laird's chair and gently sits her down. THOMAS watches, smiling, then is overcome by a fit of coughing. JENNET gives him a worried look.*)

JENNET: Thomas?

(*THOMAS tries to straighten, then collapses. JENNET supports him over to the Laird's chair.*)

MICHAEL: Ach! What ails him this time?

JENNET: (*Feeling THOMAS's forehead.*) Fever.

MICHAEL: Aye. He's been babbling, right enough.

(*MICHAEL paces while JENNET tends to THOMAS, fetching a small wooden medicine chest and opening it up.*) Rambling on about fighting dogs.

JENNET: Now, let's see. I thought I had… Ah, dried all-heal, heart o' the earth. Could you take a little, boiled in milk with butter?

(*THOMAS says something inaudible. JENNET leans forward to listen.*)

MICHAEL: What? What did he say?

(*JENNET steps away from THOMAS and turns to look at MICHAEL.*)

JENNET: He said, 'They are coming…'

Scene 8

CLEM suddenly shouts, off-stage.

CLEM: (*Off.*) Father!

MICHAEL: Here.

> (*CLEM bursts in and throws a bundle of clothes and household goods onto the floor. He is out of breath and clearly angry. MARGARET hurries on-stage after him.*)

CLEM: There's news –

> (*CLEM stops as he sees THOMAS sitting in the Laird's chair. His anger intensifies.*)

MICHAEL: What news?

CLEM: Is this the way of things? The pledge in the Laird's chair while the Laird stands tae attention?

JENNET: He is sick.

MARGARET: What ails him?

THOMAS: A little water on the lungs, Lady.

MICHAEL: (*To CLEM.*) Your news.

MARGARET: (*To CLEM.*) Why back so soon? Is all the black mail collected?

MICHAEL: Mother! Be quiet!

CLEM: (*To MICHAEL.*) I was dealing with Archie's Meg, and she –

JENNET: Dealing with her? Clem, what did you do?

> (*JENNET hurries over to the bundle and begins to look through it.*)

CLEM: (*Impatient with JENNET.*) The woman owed black mail. (*To MICHAEL.*) She said –

JENNET: Is this her insight? Clem, she is not long widowed –

CLEM: Aye, but her fields still grew a harvest this year. She could pay.

MICHAEL: What did Meg say?

JENNET: *Lifting two small coats from the bundle.* Oh, not the bairns' coats! Michael, the bairns' coats –

MICHAEL: Jennet…!

CLEM: They'll be warm enough. I left a good fire.

JENNET: You didnae. You burned them out? Michael…

> (*JENNET looks at MICHAEL pleadingly.*)

MICHAEL: Mother of God! All right! (*Turning to CLEM.*) Is this the first time she missed payment?

CLEM: If they dinnae fear us, they willnae pay.

MARGARET: (*With pride.*) Just like his grandfather.

MICHAEL: (*To CLEM.*) Aye, and why do they pay? For our protection. Protection against those who would burn them out and take their belongings!

CLEM: Father, you gave me management of the black mail.

MICHAEL: Aye, but –

CLEM: But what? I bring home more than you ever did?

(*MICHAEL turns on CLEM, who stands his ground.*)

MICHAEL: More, but not all, I hear. (*A moment of confrontation. MICHAEL turns away first.*) Away to hell! Enough of this!

JENNET: Michael – !

(*MICHAEL holds up his hand to stop JENNET's protests.*)

MICHAEL: Your news.

CLEM: It was Archie's Meg. As I burned her house, she shouted, 'You next!'

MICHAEL: You next? Like the lad at the ford. What did she mean?

CLEM: She wouldnae say at first, so I – pressed her. She told that last night the King led a raid into Teviotdale.

MICHAEL: The King!

(*MICHAEL looks over at THOMAS but he is sinking into a delirium.*)

CLEM: Aye. Our own James. He burned them out of their valley. Half of them dead, their peles destroyed and all their harvest store turned to cinders.

MARGARET: (*To JENNET.*) And you would have us be farmers!

THOMAS: (*Rambling.*) The Laird is killing the fighting dogs.

MICHAEL: (*Staring at THOMAS but talking to CLEM.*) How big a force?

CLEM: Too big for us. The King's own troops and all the Warden's men.

MICHAEL: Leaving our part of the border as quiet as the grave. And us thinking we had a charmed night.

JENNET: The King willnae attack our valley –

CLEM: You know this, do you, mother? You have spoken with him?

JENNET: (*To MICHAEL.*) He has no reason.

CLEM: We are next, father. We have no choice. We must fight. An ambush! If we take hostages we can still survive.

MICHAEL: (*To THOMAS.*) You and your bloody dogs!

JENNET: We must leave here. Hide deep in the forest where they cannae find us –

MARGARET: No! Your peace-making and promises have failed, Michael. (*Pointing to THOMAS.*) Ride to his brothers! A life for a life!

JENNET: If we start up the feud again, we give the King reason to attack us –

MARGARET: He is marching towards us even as you prattle of peace! I say we ride.

JENNET: No.

MARGARET: Ride, for your father's name –

MICHAEL: Quiet!

(*Pause.*)

We shall do neither.

(*He holds up his hands as both women get ready to start again. He points at JENNET.*)

You cannae spend a night in the forest. Nor will I feud, mother. Only a fool would leave the valley undefended now.

(*MICHAEL begins to put on his reiver armour.*)

CLEM: An ambush, then –

MICHAEL: No! We stay here, in our homes, like law abiding folk.

JENNET: (*Fearful.*) In the Devil's Ground?

MARGARET: You would have us cower in our bed-chambers until they smoke us out?

MICHAEL: If the King dares ride into this valley tonight, we shall be ready. I will fight then, mother, never fear! But – he may not come to us. A year of keeping faith with the Warden must count for something.

MARGARET: Your father –

MICHAEL: I am the Laird now!

(*MICHAEL stares MARGARET down, then turns to CLEM.*)

Clem. Go and choose men for the watches. I want beacons set all along the valley. Older, steady men, mind. And send the good, fighting men up to me.

(*CLEM exits.*)

MICHAEL: Mother. Supplies. Enough to withstand a siege. Beasts tethered, grain –

MARGARET: I know what to do.

(*MARGARET exits. MICHAEL watches her go, shaking his head, then turns to JENNET.*)

MICHAEL: Jennet, you will –

JENNET: I will get him to his bed. (*She hauls THOMAS to his feet and helps him over to the bed in the corner, closing the curtains around him.*)

MICHAEL: When he is settled, go down and oversee the women and bairns. You take each to their place for the night as they arrive. That way, there'll be no squabbling.

JENNET: And where do you go?

MICHAEL: To see to my men.

(*He is about to rush off, but JENNET calls him back.*)

JENNET: Michael…

(*They move together for a moment of tenderness, then MICHAEL exits.*)

Scene 9

JENNET walks to the window and watches for MICHAEL.

JENNET: Ah! There he goes. (*She half-raises her hand to wave, then lowers it again.*) He is busy, your father. (*She looks down at her hands as they cup her belly.*) Will you be like him? I hope so. He is a good man – and he is doing the bravest thing. He is changing. For you. He will do it, I know he can. If only we have a quiet night… Ach, it will be quiet! As quiet as the grave –

(*She falters, looks behind her at the weapons on the wall, then begins to talk again, defiantly choosing life and sexuality as a weapon against death and ghosts.*)

I know which night you were got. Oh, yes. A harvest night.
Harvest. We had been out in the fields all day. It was so
good to breathe fresh air again, instead of snatching what
sun I could from the roof of this pele. And the space…
Aye, that was the night. I am sure of it. Michael – (*She
smiles.*) – Michael was so…

Ach, well. You will bring us peace, I think. Aye, you will
be a lucky bairn. You will play in the sun. You willnae go
short of food. And when you are baptized, we shall not
leave your sword arm unchristened. Oh no. Those times
will be over. Your father will be here to watch you grow.
And Clem – and Clem…

(*JENNET looks around fearfully, then hesitantly
continues, now talking to herself as much as to the baby.*)
Clem had a brother once. His name was John. He was such a
lad! As straight as a willow wand and eyes sae clear you could
see right into his soul.

I always knew what *he* was thinking.

Clem, now…

Clem and John went out one day – and only Clem came back.
(*JENNET pauses, frowning, thinking hard. CLEM
appears silently behind her.*)

Scene 10

JENNET: (*To her baby.*) We shall have to be watchful, you and
    I.
CLEM: Watchful?
    (*JENNET turns, startled.*)
JENNET: I – I meant… Tonight.
CLEM: Ah. Tonight.
JENNET: Are the beacon watches set?
CLEM: Aye.
JENNET: All of them?
CLEM: Every one.
JENNET: But – you are back so soon.
CLEM: (*Sneering.*) I didnae go! I have men to run errands.
JENNET: Your father meant you to ride –
CLEM: My father has no sense of our position here.

JENNET: Clem, do you not see? The beacon watch is a
lonely task. A few words to each man from the Laird's son
wouldhae made such a difference. You shouldhae gone –
CLEM: You want me to go? How far away do you want,
mother? How far?
JENNET: Oh, Clem!

(*CLEM turns his back and sits down on a kist. JENNET
moves up behind him, reaches out, hesitates, then rests her
hand on his head. When CLEM does not object, she begins
to smooth his hair back from his forehead. CLEM closes his
eyes, then lets his head lean back against her. For a short
while they are content together.*)

You loved me to do this when you were a bairn. Do you
remember?

(*CLEM's eyes snap open. He pulls away.*)

CLEM: Not me.
JENNET: Aye. You did.
CLEM: It was never me.
JENNET: Have you forgot? You'd come and push your head
into my hand like a wee puppy –

(*CLEM jumps to his feet, keeping his head turned away
from JENNET so that she cannot see his anguished
expression.*)

CLEM: John. That was John.
JENNET: You too –
CLEM: No. Only John. Always John.

(*CLEM moves away from his mother.*)

JENNET: Are you sure? I thought…

(*CLEM gives no answer.*)

Do you miss him at all, Clem?
CLEM: I leave that to you.
JENNET: That day. You didnae cry. Not a tear… (*No answer.*)
Fourteen. He was fourteen…

(*JENNET finally asks the question she most wants
answered. She asks again and again, trying to break through
the distant monotone CLEM uses to re-tell a story told many
times before. She starts by stroking his arm coaxingly, but by
the end of the conversation she is hitting him.*)

What happened, Clem?

CLEM: You know –

JENNET: Tell me.

CLEM: We were racing.

JENNET: Tell me the truth!

CLEM: He had the better horse. He was –

JENNET: He loved you! His big brother –

CLEM: – way ahead. By the time I caught up, it was done. John was killed, his horse taken.

JENNET: Who killed him?

CLEM: An outlaw band. Broken men. From the Debatable Lands.

JENNET: He loved you!

CLEM: I could see them, when I reached him. Way ahead, little dots, riding fast –

(*JENNET begins to thump CLEM on the back and shoulders.*)

JENNET: Who killed him, Clem!

(*CLEM snaps out of the story and turns on JENNET.*)

CLEM: Say it! Say what you think!

JENNET: (*Softly, after a pause.*) Why did you hate him?

(*CLEM struggles with himself, as though he is about to say something important.*)

CLEM: I…

(*Then THOMAS calls out in his fever.*)

THOMAS: Mother!

(*JENNET hurries toward the bed chamber. CLEM turns away. JENNET looks back to CLEM, torn, but she has lost him. She leaves to tend to THOMAS. Left alone, CLEM throws himself into the Laird's chair. The Devil's Music builds as the apparition of the Devil o' the Moss appears. MARGARET's voice is mixed in with the music, repeating the phrases she used to frighten JENNET.*)

MARGARET: He will walk.

He will take the weakest.

For the blood feud.

The weakest…

(*CLEM is oblivious until the apparition is standing over him. He shrinks down in the chair as the apparitions bends*) *over him. The apparition straightens and exits, leaving CLEM doubled over in the chair. Slowly CLEM raises his head. His face is a skull. He is possessed by the Devil o'the Moss. The lights go down.*)

End Of Act One.

ACT TWO

Scene 1

It is night in the pele. Moonlight shines through the window, marking out the bars on the floor. THOMAS still lies in the bed, with the curtains drawn around him. Off-stage, MICHAEL, CLEM, MARGARET and JENNET begin to sing the border ballad The Wife of Usher's Well in close harmony.

Everything – everyone – is in place. Now the waiting watch begins. The singing continues as the four come on stage one by one.

CLEM is first. He looks no different but his behaviour is cold and distant. He moves to the far side of the stage and lounges, polishing his sword.

JENNET enters next, catching a coldly hostile glance from CLEM. She positions herself as though looking from the window.

MARGARET is third, taking her husband's dagger from the display as she passes.

Last is MICHAEL. He is in full reiver armour and carries a Jeddart staff.

Still singing, they stand watch, seeing how the night goes, waiting for the flare of beacons, for any sign of attack. They stay like this until the ballad is finished. In the silence following the song, they stay alert and still, looking. Slowly, the lights come up. They look to one another. Finally, MICHAEL nods, then stretches and moves to rest his staff against the chair.

Scene 2

MICHAEL: They will not come now. We are safe.

MARGARET: Safe! Safety is for sheep! Your father –

MICHAEL: Is dead! He is dead, mother, and his way of life with him. Do you hear me? You can put his dagger back in its place now. There will be no more blood feud. This night, this *peaceful* night, has shown that my way is right.

MARGARET: You mean weak –

JENNET: Strong! It takes strength to try a new way.

MARGARET: (*To MICHAEL.*) You will need your strength when she puts you into harness.

MICHAEL: Mother!

(*MARGARET turns her back on him, returns the dagger to the display and takes down the standard.*)

CLEM: We are to be farmers?

MARGARET: (*Holding the standard out to MICHAEL.*) Here. Bury this in the first field you plough.

CLEM: Are we?

MICHAEL: Put it back, mother.

MARGARET: No! I'll not have a corpse on display.

MICHAEL: A corpse?

MARGARET: Our name. You and your new way – you will kill it.

CLEM: Are we?

JENNET: (*To MARGARET.*) How can you say that? (*She sweeps her arm to take in MICHAEL and CLEM.*) They willnae die now.

MARGARET: Oh, they will die, when they are old or tired enough.

JENNET: I mean they willnae have to die for the name.

MARGARET: Then what a weary waste their deaths will be. To die for nothing! The name means more than a few lives –

JENNET: A few lives! Our sons!

MARGARET: Our family has carried this (*Pushing the standard into JENNET's face.*) with honour for generations.

JENNET: Aye, and look at it. Sae steeped in blood and dirt, ye cannae see what lies beneath.

MARGARET: We have nae need to see. We know what is there.

MICHAEL: (*Taking the standard and returning it to the display.*) That's enough. I'm tired. I want some peace.

MARGARET: Peace, is it? The Devil o' the Moss is not at peace.

(JENNET reacts with fear and makes the sign of the cross. CLEM becomes very still. MARGARET does not notice, she is venting her anger on JENNET.)

He is walking. Soon he will reach the pele. Soon you will hear his heel bones, scraping on the stone behind you. Soon you will catch the stench of him. Dirt and rot – do you smell it? He will take the weakest –

JENNET: You are an evil old woman!

(JENNET's shout breaks CLEM's trance.)

MARGARET: Shall I call him up? Aye, maybe I will call him.

JENNET: An evil, jealous old woman!

MICHAEL: Leave her, Jennet. It is only talk.

(JENNET gives him a look. He turns away, losing patience, and heads off-stage.)

Talk…talk… There is ower much talk in this peace business.

JENNET: Don't go…

MICHAEL: They will expect to see me riding in the valley today. You know that.

JENNET: I only meant – *(She looks fearfully at MARGARET and at the display of weapons.)* – don't go yet. You need food – and rest –

MICHAEL: Rest? Here? *(He looks at JENNET and relents slightly.)* I'll be back by nightfall. You should rest. Go to bed. Sleep.

JENNET: No. I must sit with Thomas. His fever is worse.

(MICHAEL returns to JENNET and, standing so that he blocks CLEM and MARGARET's view, he rests his hand on her belly.)

MICHAEL: It isnae a catching fever? *(JENNET smiles and shakes her head.)* Good.

(CLEM makes a disgusted noise. MICHAEL gives him a sharp look, then kicks the bundle of household goods belonging to Archie's Meg.)

Clem. Take this back to Archie's Meg.

CLEM: What!

MICHAEL: Do as I tell you.

CLEM: You gave the black mail to me.

MICHAEL: Aye. I did. I had no taste for it. But you. You have taken to it ower well. You must curb your methods now. They dinnae fit the times.

(*CLEM and MARGARET exchange looks. CLEM picks up the bundle and moves away from MICHAEL. JENNET leaves the main room, going behind the screens around the bed to tend to THOMAS. MICHAEL heads off-stage, but stops when, behind him, CLEM throws down the bundle of clothes.*)

MICHAEL: Clem!

(*CLEM turns defiantly. MICHAEL points at the bundle.*) To Meg.

CLEM: She is nothing! She is not of our name!

(*MICHAEL grabs the bundle and shoves it into CLEM's chest. CLEM nearly falls.*)

MICHAEL: Take it back!

(*MICHAEL exits.*)

Scene 3

CLEM and MARGARET are left alone. CLEM throws down the bundle, coldly furious.

MARGARET: See? Soft. I warned you.

(*CLEM kicks the bundle to one side, then goes to the display of weapons. MARGARET trails him, still talking.*) Take us back to solid ground, Clem. Start the feud anew. Ride with your men –

(*CLEM whirls to face her. He holds the dagger of the Devil o' the Moss.*)

CLEM: And what happens to me? Have you thought of that? There will be no place for me here if I do as you want.

(*MARGARET flinches back, but recovers quickly. By the time CLEM has secured the dagger at his belt, she is onto him again.*)

MARGARET: You think you are apart from all this? Your men are loyal only while the black mail pays. When they hear of you carrying insight back to a tenant woman like a bairn on an errand –

CLEM: My father will forget about Meg's insight soon
enough. He'll have other things on his mind.
(*As CLEM reveals his plan to MARGARET, JENNET
leaves the bed chamber with an empty water jug. She backs
into the shadows and listens with growing horror as she
realizes what her son is planning to do.*)

MARGARET: Tell me.

CLEM: The pledge will escape.

MARGARET: Ach! That spying runt? He didnae have the
guts when he was well. Now he is ill –

CLEM: He will escape. I will make sure of it.

MARGARET: You – ? (*Understanding.*) When?

CLEM: This afternoon, while my father is out of the way. You
will call my mother away from his bedside to –

MARGARET: To go and check the stores with me?

CLEM: Aye. That'll do. I'll take him then.

MARGARET: Where?

CLEM: There are many places in the valley where a body
could be hidden. He'll not be found. The truce will be
broken.

MARGARET: But, even then, if she has her way –

CLEM: The feud *shall* start again. If my father willnae ride,
then the pledge's brothers surely will.

MARGARET: They think nothing of him!

CLEM: Alive, no. But when I deliver his murdered body to
their door –

MARGARET: They'll be honour bound to avenge him.

CLEM: Then there'll be no more talk of farming.
(*Together, CLEM and MARGARET exit.*)

Scene 4

*JENNET runs to the bed and pulls back the curtains. She shakes
THOMAS.*

JENNET: Thomas? Wake up. You must hide. You must…
(*THOMAS does not respond.*)
Thomas! For my laird's sake. For my bairn's sake.
Please…!

(*JENNET stops trying to wake THOMAS and sinks to the bed, defeated.*) For my bairn…
(*She reaches over to stroke THOMAS's hair from his face.*)
Bairns. What happens tae them, hmmm? A' the laughing and the softness, the clean smell of them… (*She breathes in, remembering.*) Sun-warmed skin. And the back of their necks – their wee necks – flower stalks… Stalks for legs, too! All arms and legs, they are! And growing faster than a body can sew… Oh, the beauty of them.
What happens…?
Feud and famine. A' their softness cut away. A' their laughing hushed…
(*She straightens up, determined.*)
No. We'll not have feud again. Wake up, Thomas. You must hide, or he'll take you. He'll take you out with him and you'll not come back – he's done it before…!
(*She stands and looks down at THOMAS.*)
I'll not let it happen again.
(*She begins to rearrange THOMAS on the bed, smoothing the bed covers, laying him out as though he is already dead.*)
He shallnae have you. I'll keep you here. I'll keep you safe.
(*She moves through to the main room, takes the length of silk from the back of the chair. She is in an almost trance-like state.*)
For my laird's sake. For my bairn's sake. (*Slowly, methodically, she folds the length of silk.*) He died of a fever. Not a mark on him. Aye. He was always sickly. A wonder he lived sae long. (*She finishes folding the silk into a pad the size of a small pillow.*)
Aye, a fever. His chest filled up. No air. No one's fault. Here's the body for the Warden, see? Look at the face, not a mark on it!
(*She looks down at the silk pad, rests it on the palm of her hand, presses the other hand down onto it.*)
Silk willnae bruise. Silk is sae soft. Soft against the skin…
(*THOMAS's tune begins to play as JENNET goes to the bed, closing the curtains behind her. The lights go down. The melody plays on in the darkness until the last few notes die away.*)

Scene 5

When the lights go up again, JENNET is outside the curtains, but slumped against the bed. She has been guarding THOMAS's body but has fallen asleep. It is later in the day. THOMAS's bed chamber is in darkness, the curtains closed. MICHAEL enters, still in full armour and tired from his day of riding. He goes over to JENNET and lays his hand on her head. JENNET erupts from the floor, screaming.

JENNET: Get away! You shallnae have him!
> (*MARGARET hurries onstage. JENNET backs away from her, arms outstretched to stop her from entering the bed chamber.*)

MICHAEL: What in hell is going on here?

JENNET: Michael –

MARGARET: She willnae let us near. She is –

MICHAEL: What? She is what?

MARGARET: Possessed.
> (*MICHAEL catches JENNET as she falls into his arms.*)

JENNET: I couldnae leave him. Not 'til you came back.

MARGARET: All day, she wouldnae let us near –

JENNET: The fever took him –

MICHAEL: Clem…?

MARGARET: Nay. The pledge.

MICHAEL: The pledge is dead?

JENNET: (*With fury.*) Thomas! His name is Thomas!
> (*MICHAEL attempts to calm JENNET but she dances away from him, on the edge of hysteria.*)
> He died of a fever. Not a mark on him

MICHAEL: (*Calming.*) Ach. That is a shame. You did your best, Jennet. His life was yours.

JENNET: Mine?

MICHAEL: He wouldhae been dead months back but for you. He was a sickly wee get.

JENNET: Aye! He was always sickly. A wonder he lives sae long. A fever –

MICHAEL: I know. You said…

JENNET: – No air. No one's fault. (*She points to the curtained bed-chamber.*) – There's the body for the Warden. Go and see. Look at the face. Not a mark on it!

MICHAEL: First, you must sit down –

JENNET: Go! You must see the body!

MICHAEL: All right. All right…

JENNET: He looks as peaceful as a sleeping bairn.

(*MICHAEL heads for the curtained bed chamber and disappears inside. Behind the curtain, he begins to laugh. He steps out again.*)

MICHAEL: Like a sleeping bairn, you said? Well, that is what he was doing!

JENNET: What?

MICHAEL: Sleeping! He wasnae dead at all.

JENNET: (*Horrified.*) He is breathing?

MICHAEL: He must be breathing, wherever he is. He wouldnae get far otherwise.

MARGARET: The pledge has gone?

(*MICHAEL pulls back the curtains to show the empty bed.*)

JENNET: No. No, he was dead! I know he was because I –

(*JENNET stops and looks around, suddenly realizing that CLEM is missing.*)

Clem. Where is Clem?

MICHAEL: He'll not be far –

JENNET: (*Desperate.*) I promised him I'd keep him safe.

MICHAEL: (*Misunderstanding.*) Clem is fine –

JENNET: No! Where is he!

MICHAEL: (*To MARGARET.*) Find him.

(*To JENNET.*) Clem can look after himself –

JENNET: Clem!

(*CLEM enters. JENNET rushes at him.*)

Where is he?

CLEM: Who?

JENNET: You've taken him. I know.

MICHAEL: (*Still misunderstanding.*) This is Clem, Jennet. He is here.

JENNET: And John? Where is he?

MICHAEL: Does she mean the pledge?

MARGARET: See? Possessed.

JENNET: (*To CLEM.*) Not far. I didnae sleep long. You can't have taken him far in such a short time. Tell me!

CLEM: What is happening?

MARGARET: The pledge has escaped. The truce is broken.

(*JENNET stares at MARGARET, shakes her head. She staggers and MICHAEL catches her up.*)

Scene 6

MICHAEL: Help me with her.

(*CLEM takes JENNET's other arm. They take her to the bed and lie her down.*)

Let her sleep. That's all she needs, after last night.

MARGARET: Now will you ride?

MICHAEL: Mother, do you ne'er give up?

MARGARET: The pledge has escaped –

MICHAEL: Escaped? Barefoot, in his shift? He's wandering in a fever more like.

CLEM: He's gone. It doesnae matter why. He has given us a reason to ride, if you will take it.

MICHAEL: No. The truce holds. I willnae ride. (*Wearily.*) But I will go out and find the lad before the cold finishes him off.

(*MICHAEL starts for the door but stops as he notices MEG's bundle still in the corner. He kicks the bundle towards CLEM.*)

Still here.

CLEM: Father –

MICHAEL: It is still here!

CLEM: You cannae make me take it –

MICHAEL: I am the Laird.

CLEM: But, my men –

MICHAEL: Your men! We'll see how long that rabble stays with you when you have no black mail to collect.

CLEM: You cannae –

MICHAEL: Cannae again is it? The next time black mail's due, it'll be Andrew's Jock collecting it.

CLEM: He willnae match me.

MICHAEL: Aye. Mebbe not. But I dinnae like your methods, son. Power turns awful sour when there is no heart to sweeten it. Now. Will you take Meg's insight back to her?
(*CLEM looks across at his grandmother and MICHAEL loses his temper at last. He hits or pushes CLEM.*)
You look to her for an answer?
(*MICHAEL glares at them both, then walks to the door. He turns, points at them.*)
There will be changes here...
(*MICHAEL exits.*)

CLEM: He cannae...

MARGARET: He just did. I didnae see you stopping him.

CLEM: I willnae do it. I would sooner live with the broken men in the Debatable Lands.

MARGARET: Are those the only choices you see? To do as you are told or run away? For a while there, I thought I could see something of your grandfather... Ach, away! Leave me be!
(*CLEM exits.*)

Scene 7

MARGARET looks across at the standard.

MARGARET: And you. You! How can the Devil o'the Moss lie sae quiet in such – peacable – times? We are grown so small with you gone. The feud is lost. Your son willnae fight for you! And your grandson...

Do you hear me? If the living willnae save our name, then the dead must. Come back, do you hear? Walk! Scrape the dirt from your eye sockets and walk!
(*A shadowy, cloaked and hooded figure moves onto the stage behind MARGARET.*)
Let them see the Devil o' the Moss forced from his grave for the honour of his name. Let them see the Devil walk, with beetles crushed between his jaws and each rib laced with worms!

Just the once.

Once would be enough! They'd fight your feud after that, for fear of seeing you again!

Ach, what's the use? It is finished. I know it is finished, but I cannae stop.

Because you! You left me nothing else.

They have love, your son and her. They love…

(*The Devil's Music starts up and MARGARET turns, finally aware that there is something behind her. She stares at the skull face of the apparition and prepares to run, but the figure makes no attempt to follow, only holds out its hands to her. Fearful yet also moved, MARGARET steps forward and takes the figure's hands. They turn slowly, once, twice, in the beginnings of a dance. The figure pulls MARGARET closer. She acquiesces at first, even welcomes the embrace but as the turning dance and the Devil's Music gradually grow wilder, she begins to struggle, trying to escape. She cannot, the dance and the music are out of control now. One last turn and the figure raises the dagger of the Devil o' the Moss, plunging it down as he whirls MARGARET off the stage. The Devil's Music stops as MARGARET, off-stage, gives one, agonized cry.*)

Scene 8

JENNET is still asleep in the bed. The moonlight shines through the muslin curtains onto her face. THOMAS's fiddle tune begins to play, quietly, sadly, as he glides on stage. She is dreaming him. What follows is like a duet, a ritualized mourning.

JENNET: (*Still sleeping.*) John…?

THOMAS: The sons dying, the mothers crying. Always the same.

JENNET: John…

THOMAS: Always. A great chain of them. Mothers crying. Sons dying. Always.

(*THOMAS moves to stand at her head, looking down at her. She begins to stir. He backs away and drifts off-stage as she sits up in the bed. The fiddle tune fades.*)

JENNET: (*This time, hopeful.*) John…? (*Her hopeful expression changes to one of grief as she sees the empty room.*) Always the same.

Scene 9

Now fully awake, JENNET realizes she is in the bed where THOMAS died. She leaps from the bed, backing off into the main room. She turns to the door as MICHAEL enters. He is carrying the distinctive, blood-stained dagger of the Devil o' the Moss.

MICHAEL: My mother. My mother is dead. Lying on his grave. Bleeding on my father's grave.

JENNET: She called him up! She said she would. She called and he came. He killed her.

MICHAEL: A fetch cannae hold a dagger!

JENNET: She took her own life?

MICHAEL: Never! (*He stops, coming to a realization.*) It was the pledge.

JENNET: No. Not Thomas.

MICHAEL: Who else? (*He begins to search the room.*) That's why I couldnae find him outside the walls. He was here in the pele all the time! Hiding. Biding his time. Waiting for his chance.

JENNET: It couldnae be Thomas.

MICHAEL: Waiting for our trust. After a year with us. A year! He used my father's dagger. The sly bastard! He is as evil as his murdering brothers!

JENNET: Michael. Thomas didnae murder her.

MICHAEL: Nae more soft talk. We were wrong. Peace is not for us. My mother is killed and I must ride.

JENNET: Thomas couldnae. He is dead. I killed him. I smothered him in that bed.

(*MICHAEL stares at her, then shakes his head.*)

MICHAEL: You didnae. There is no body.

JENNET: Clem has hid it.

MICHAEL: Why would he…?

JENNET: To make you think Thomas had escaped. To make you ride.

MICHAEL: You? Killed?

JENNET: Aye. To keep the truce…

MICHAEL: You killed? With a bairn inside you?

JENNET: Do I lie? To you?

(*MICHAEL stares at her as though she has turned from a rose to a snake in front of his eyes. He backs off when she tries to touch him.*)

MICHAEL: Why?

JENNET: For you –

MICHAEL: Me! You killed for me?

JENNET: For peace –

MICHAEL: You were my peace!

JENNET: Michael –

MICHAEL: A' for you. A' the talk. A' the truce-making –

JENNET: Please!

MICHAEL: (*Every word torn out of him.*) Do you know what you have done?

Scene 10

CLEM walks on in a daze. He holds out his hands. They are covered in blood.

CLEM: Mother?

(*JENNET rushes to him, thinking he is hurt.*)

JENNET: Clem! What happened? (*She examines him but can find no wounds.*) But – you are not hurt –

CLEM: I had the dagger… Then I lost it…

(*A stillness comes over the room. JENNET looks at MICHAEL. CLEM follows her gaze as, slowly, MICHAEL lifts his hand, displaying the dagger. CLEM is still struggling with a memory which will not come clear.*) Where did you find it?

MICHAEL: Next to my mother's body.

(*CLEM looks down at his hands.*)

CLEM: …I… Killed her…?

(*With a roar of pain, MICHAEL charges CLEM, unsheathing his sword as he goes. A furious fight ensues. CLEM, confused and shocked, is at first very much on the defensive but gradually begins to fight back. MICHAEL – fighting out of rage and hurt – is not thinking tactically. As CLEM's head clears he becomes the stronger fighter. He first wounds MICHAEL in the arm, then catches him off-*

balance. As MICHAEL falls to his knees, CLEM moves behind him, gripping him under the chin and holding the edge of his sword to MICHAEL's throat. Poised to kill his father, CLEM is very dangerous, because he is distressed, frightened and angry all at once.)

JENNET: Clem! Dinnae hurt him. Clem, please…

(*She takes a step towards CLEM. He brings his sword up, digging further into MICHAEL's throat.*)

Clem! It wasnae you killed her, do you ken? Your hands, aye. But not you.

CLEM: (*Vaguely.*) The Devil o' the Moss…?

JENNET: She called him up. He possessed you –

CLEM: She said he would take the weakest. She was right!

JENNET: Oh, Clem. Not weak…

(*CLEM drops his sword and MICHAEL collapses to the floor.*)

CLEM: John wasnae winning. He wasnae way ahead. We were together as we rounded the big rock.

It was a grand race! We were shouting with the thrill of it! Blue sky wheeling – peewits shrieking high – the smell of horse sweat…

I couldnae tell which was beating faster, my heart or their hooves. We rounded the big rock, neck and neck –

They were waiting for us there.

Ambush.

I was – I was awful feared. But John, he didnae flinch.

They ringed us. A' with swords. The blades! Nicked and marked with use.

He didnae flinch.

They laughed, when he drew his sword.

He went for the one who was laughing hardest. Carved a gap!

Their faces slack with the shock of it…

John carved a gap, but didnae take it.

He carved a gap and held it…

'Ride! Ride Clem!'

I did.

God help me, I rode.

They didnae chase me. Their horses were near-starved. That's why they wanted ours.

When I looked back, all I could see were their blades, rising and falling, rising and falling. Flashing at first, the steel. Then, after a time, no brightness left for the sun to catch.

A' the brightness gone...

JENNET: Oh, my Clem. My bairn. I thought –

CLEM: I let you think it. This was worse.

JENNET: Not to me.

> (*CLEM runs off-stage, unable to bear the loving expression on his mother's face.*)
> Clem!

Scene 11

MICHAEL struggles to his feet. JENNET goes to help him, but he refuses her hand and makes his own way to his chair. JENNET tries to look at his wound, but he turns her away again.

MICHAEL: Will he kill us all?

JENNET: He only practices what he has learned.

MICHAEL: Like the rest of us.

> (*THOMAS appears, standing at MICHAEL's head. MICHAEL and JENNET cannot see him and only MICHAEL can hear THOMAS's voice, as though it is in his own head. JENNET can only hear MICHAEL's voice.*)

THOMAS: And what if the dogs change – what then?

MICHAEL: Fighting dogs cannae change. It is in their nature to attack.

THOMAS: Then the Laird will kill them. They must change, or die. Do you ken?

MICHAEL: Or die...

> (*MICHAEL's head falls back. His eyes close. He is exhausted. JENNET goes to his side, stroking his hair as he sleeps, finally allowed to touch him. THOMAS moves to stand behind JENNET, watching her unseen. When THOMAS speaks, she does not hear him, but believes the idea has come from her own head.*)

THOMAS: You can still make this right.

JENNET: I can still make this right. If I can find Thomas and lay him out on his sick-bed for the warden to see, there is still a chance for peace. Where are you Thomas…?

(*JENNET begins searching for THOMAS. She does not hear him when he guides her, but believes she is following her own intuition.*)

THOMAS: Look. Do you see me? Out there. Do you see me?

(*JENNET moves to the window that looks out over the drowning hole. The reflections of the water ripple across her face.*)

JENNET: Where, Thomas. Where?

THOMAS: Can you see where he hid me? Cold and quiet. Floating. Peace.

JENNET: The drowning hole…?

(*THOMAS smiles, bows his head and walks off.*)

The drowning hole!

Scene 12

JENNET turns to look at MICHAEL who is beginning to stir. She turns back to the window as the light turns to a flickering red. She reacts with shock as the red light grows stronger. She runs to MICHAEL and shakes him awake.

JENNET: Michael!

MICHAEL: What?

JENNET: Beacons! Bale fires all along the valley!

(*MICHAEL stumbles to the window and stares out.*)

MICHAEL: The King comes after all. So, that is to be the way of it. The dogs cannae change, for the Laird will not let them.

(*MICHAEL painfully begins to fasten up his jack, collect his helmet and sword, etc.*)

JENNET: Michael, wait. If it is the raid, if it is the boy killed at the ford, you could still talk –

MICHAEL: The reason doesnae matter. They are here.

(*CLEM bursts in. MICHAEL draws his sword. CLEM holds up his hands.*)

CLEM: Father, the King –

MICHAEL: – is raiding. I know.

CLEM: More than that. The warden too.

MICHAEL: Aye.

CLEM: And alongside the warden –

MICHAEL: Who?

CLEM: Their standard and his – (*Bringing his hands together.*) That close.

JENNET: Thomas's brothers…

CLEM: In open alliance.

MICHAEL: (*Lowering his sword.*) We are betrayed.

CLEM: Aye.

JENNET: Not Thomas. He didnae know of this. He couldnae…

MICHAEL: Still, he played his part. A pledge to keep us quiet. (*Turning on CLEM and raising his sword again.*) And you? What do you want here?

CLEM: I would fight.

MICHAEL: Them? Or me?

CLEM: Father…

(*MICHAEL lowers his sword, turns to the window. CLEM moves to stand beside him.*)

MICHAEL: There is only one, clear path to take. We must fight now, for our name's sake. We will meet them on the Devil's Ground and they will not find us easy prey.

CLEM: Here they come!

MICHAEL: Let's see the size of them. We may be able to…

(*CLEM and MICHAEL watch as the attacking force comes into view. Their faces change as they see the numbers they have to face. Their eyes scan the valley from side to side, then they turn to look at one another. JENNET, aware of the silence, lifts her head.*)

JENNET: What? What is it?

(*She tries to see, but MICHAEL swings her away from the window to face him.*)

MICHAEL: A rabble! Not worth looking at!

JENNET: Michael –

MICHAEL: Shhh! Still my peace. Always my peace.

(*They stare into one another's eyes, intense. MICHAEL turns to CLEM.*)

The standard.

(*CLEM takes it from the wall, holds it out to his father, but MICHAEL pushes it back to him. CLEM straightens, holding the standard.*)

JENNET: One harvest. That was all. This land has forgot the shape of peace.

MICHAEL: Jennet! This will be a night for the ballads! (*He smiles.*) They never sing of farmers.

(*They are busy now, getting ready. JENNET helps, moving between them, fastening buckles, brushing down shoulders.*)

JENNET: Promise me –

MICHAEL: Aye?

JENNET: When you come back – we will leave the Devil's Ground. You, me, Clem, the bairn. Promise me we'll go. All of us.

MICHAEL: (*Nodding seriously.*) When we get back.

JENNET: (*Nodding too.*) When you get back.

(*MICHAEL and JENNET kiss. CLEM and JENNET embrace.*)

MICHAEL: Bar the door behind us. Close the shutters. (*Putting his hand to her belly.*) Tell him, how I fought.

(*MICHAEL and CLEM exit.*)

Scene 13

JENNET goes to the window, looks out on the huge force approaching down the valley. She picks up the length of blue silk from the chair, unravels it and wraps it softly around her shoulders. She stands straight, formal, and sings The Border Widow's Lament.

When the lament is finished, she takes the silk and forms it into the shape of a baby, which she cradles in her arms. Then she lets the silk unravel into a blue pool on the floor at her feet. She stares down into the pool, then steps into it.

JENNET: Floating.

(*JENNET bends and picks up the silk, drawing it slowly up her body.*)
Is it quiet, Thomas? (*She raises the silk above her head, then lets her arms fall.*) Is it peaceful…?
(*As the noise of battle grows, JENNET turns, trailing the silk behind her. She exits the stage. The long tail of silk unwinds and follows after her, shimmering across the floor until the last corner disappears. The stage darkens as the sound of battle grows to a huge volume.*)

Scene 14

The five actors stand out of sight of the audience, each behind one of the long banners which hang from the roof down each edge of the stage. The sound of battle fades enough for them to be heard as they recite a speech of King James.

MICHAEL: We have thought good to discontinue the divided name of England and Scotland out of our Royal style and do intend to take to us the name and style of King of Great Britain.

THOMAS: The late Marches and borders of the two realms are now the heart of the country. We therefore prohibit the name of Borders any longer to be used, substituting in its place, Middle Shires.

CLEM: Proclamation is to be made against all rebels and disorderly persons that no supply be given to them, their wives or their bairns and that they be prosecuted with fire and sword.

ALL: All places of strength in these parts are to be demolished, their iron gates to be converted into plough shares and their inhabitants to betake themselves to agriculture and other works of peace.
(*Battle noises fade. Lights go down.*)

The End.

SONGS

Kinmont Willie

O have ye na heard o' the fause Sakelde?
O have ye na heard o' the keen Lord Scroope?
How they hae ta'en bauld Kinmont Willie,
On Hairibee to hang him up?

Had Willie had but twenty men,
But twenty men as stout as he,
Fause Sakelde had never the Kinmont ta'en
Wi' eight score in his companie.

They band his legs beneath the steed,
They tied his hands behind his back;
They guarded him fivesome on each side,
And they brought him over the Liddel-rack.

They led him thro' the Liddel-rack
And also thro' the Carlisle sands;
They brought him to Carlisle castell
To be at my Lord Scroope's commands.

'My hands are tied but my tongue is free,
And wha will dare this deed avow?
Or answer by the border law?
Or answer to the bauld Buccleuch?'

'Now haud thy tongue, thou rank reiver!
There's never a Scot shall set thee free;
Before ye cross my castle-yate
I trow ye shall take farewell o' me.'

The Wife of Usher's Well

There lived a wife at Usher's Well,
And a wealthy wife was she;
She had three stout and stalwart sons,
And sent them o'er the sea.

They hadna been a week from her,
A week but barely ane,
Whan word came to the carline wife,
That her three sons were gane.

They hadna been a week from her,
A week but barely three,
Whan word came to the carline wife,
That her sons she'd never see.

I wish the wind may never cease,
Nor fishes in the flood,
Till my three sons come hame to me,
In earthly flesh and blood!'

It fell about the Martinmas,
Whan nights are lang and mirk,
The carline wife's three sons came hame,
And their hats were o' the birk.

It neither grew in syke nor ditch,
Nor yet in ony sheugh;
But at the gates o' Paradise,
That birk grew fair eneugh.

'Blow up the fire, my maidens!
Bring water from the well!
For a' my house shall feast this night,
Since my three sons are well.'

And she has made to them a bed,
She's made it large and wide;
And she's ta'en her mantle her about,
Sat down at the bed-side.

*

Up then crew the red red cock,
And up and crew the gray;
The eldest to the youngest said,
'Tis time we were away.

The cock he hadna crawed but once,
And clapped his wings at a',
When the youngest to the eldest said,
'Brother, we must awa' .

The cock doth craw, the day doth daw,
The channerin' worm doth chide;
Gin we be mist out o' our place,
A sair pain we maun bide.

'Fare ye weel, my mother dear!
Fareweel to barn and byre!
And fare ye weel, the bonny lass,
That kindles my mother's fire.'

The Border Widow's Lament

My love built me a bonnie bow'r
And clad it a' wi' lily flow'r
A brawer bow'r ye ne'er did see
Than my true love he built for me.

There cam' a man by middle day,
He spied his sport and went away,
And brocht the king at dead o' night.
Who broke my bow'r and slew my knight.

He slew my knight, tae me sae dear,
He slew my knight and poin'd his gear.
My servants all for life did flee,
And left me in extremitie.

I sewed his sheet, making my mane;
I watch'd his corpse, myself alane;
I watch'd his body night and day;
No living creature cam' that way.

I took his body on my back,
An' whiles I gaed, an' whiles I sat;
I digged a grave and laid him in,
And happed him wi' the sod sae green.

But think na ye my hert was sair,
When I laid the mould on his yellow hair.
Oh think na ye my hert was wae,
When I turned aboot awa' tae gae.

Nae living man I'll love again,
Since that my lovely knight is slain.
Wi' ae lock of his yellow hair,
I'll chain my hert for evermair.